8/23

THE PASS

The Passion of God

by

ANTHONY PHILLIPS

The Canterbury Press
Norwich

© Anthony Phillips 1995
First published 1995 by The Canterbury Press Norwich
(a publishing imprint of Hymns Ancient & Modern Limited,
a registered charity)
St Mary's Works, St Mary's Plain,
Norwich, Norfolk, NR3 3BH

British Library Cataloguing in Publication Data

A catalogue record for this book is available
from the British Library

ISBN 1-85311-101-5

*Typeset by Datix International Limited
Bungay, Suffolk and
Printed and bound in Great Britain by
St Edmundsbury Press Limited
Bury St Edmunds, Suffolk*

DEDICATION

To all my pupils, but especially to the class of 1993
– Lucy, Felicity, Charlotte, Hugo, Holly, James, Duncan,
Stuart, Andrew, Neil, James, Jocelyn, William, Julian and
my daughter Lucy.

ACKNOWLEDGEMENTS

I should like to thank T. and T. Clark, publishers of the *Expository Times* for permission to republish my Macbride sermon (*ET* 90, 1979, pp. 370–4) and Bellew Press for similar permission to reproduce my contribution 'On Leaving' to *Tradition and Unity*, Ed. D. Cohn-Sherbok, London 1990

Canterbury *October 1994*   ANTHONY PHILLIPS

Contents

Preface

WHEN I was at theological college, one of the lecturers told me that a priest had at most three sermons in him. For St Paul there was one – Christ Crucified. Central to the Gospel is the cross, not the empty sign of victory over death, but the executioner's instrument with the powerless Christ nailed to it – the ultimate expression of the passion of God. This marks both the measure of God's commitment to his creation, and the invitation which of necessity his followers must accept if that commitment is to be realised. So Jesus summons his followers to take up their cross, to assume their own vocation to powerlessness. As in Gethsemane, obedience will demand going on when there appears to be no reason to go on, going on in the face of a silent God who at one's greatest point of need can remain agonisingly absent. The passion of God exercised by the Son in the absence of the Father is then the very essence of the believer's faith.

This collection of addresses celebrates these complementary truths of the Gospel – the joy in God's unimaginable love and the response that such love must evoke. Christianity is a risky business: it depends not on security, safety and self-preservation – though the established Church spends much time in attempting to ensure this: the Gospel can only take root in abandonment and self-annihilation. For on the cross, God confirmed that it is only by dying that we can live – only through death that resurrection lies. Never has St Paul's commitment to the preaching of Christ Crucified been more urgent: the future of western christendom depends on it. I hope these sermons for all their shortcomings may be of encouragement to others in this essential task.

I

BAPTISM

It is appropriate that the first address in this collection should have been preached at a Baptism. In this sacrament, the Christian commits herself or himself to Christ crucified, responds to the invitation of the passion of God. This sermon was preached at the baptism of Thomas, whose parents I had married and whose father is himself a priest.

FROM the Gospel according to St Matthew 16.24–25:

> Then Jesus told his disciples, 'If any man would come after me, let him deny himself and take up his cross and follow me. For whoever would save his life will lose it, and whoever loses his life for my sake will find it'.

I doubt if anyone can attend the baptism of an infant without some questioning about what is going on. Indeed if there has not been, then one wonders if the baptism should take place at all. Baptism is not something which can just be taken for granted, any more than the Eucharist can be taken for granted. Both sacraments are at face value odd. A baby splashed with a token drop of water; the distribution of a wafer and a sip of wine. These are held on the one hand to mark the passing from death to life, of rebirth in the family of the church; and on the other the sharing in the very body and blood of the Saviour. Outward and visible signs of inward and spiritual truths, the catechism boldly proclaims. But even the faithful have their sceptical moments. Can so much really be claimed? At least the necessity for confirma-

tion postpones the sharing in the eucharist until the age of
discretion has been reached – though the church seems
happy to treat this as an euphemism. But what about a
helpless infant? How can today's ceremony in any way
effect the child incapable of understanding one jot of what
goes on?

I cannot but sympathise with this line of questioning.
One has all too often ministered the sacrament of baptism
in circumstances which were either superstitious or sentimental. Yet even in these circumstances I wonder whether our
questioning does not spring from an improper desire to
protect God, to make sure that he will not be compromised
by what we do. But the one thing that is quite certain,
though Church people seem to find it difficult to accept, is
that God can do without our protection, is beyond being
compromised. He who created man is capable of looking
after himself. What of course in our rationalistic age we
fight shy of, is doing something which we cannot scientific-
ally explain, whose efficacy can be appropriated but not
proved. We fight shy of faith.

For what Thomas's parents will do in bringing their
infant for baptism is to affirm their faith in three ways. In
the first place they will say that the birth of their child was
more than just a human process. Like all men, he was loved
into life by God himself. He is not theirs to do with as they
like until he is old enough to look after himself. He is God's
gift to them: they are stewards of their baby, as they are
stewards of all that God has created and entrusted to their
care. Their task is to enable Thomas to fulfil himself in the
way in which God intends him to fulfil himself, enable him
to be – be whom God has destined him to be. Their care,
example, love and discipline – what the Hebrews called
wisdom – should enable him when the time comes to make
the right decisions, lead him to become himself. Of course
for the parents from the moment of his birth, it is a process
of letting go in order that he may be. At baptism they take
that first step in letting go, in acknowledging that his first

loyalty is to God, that they can only enjoy him through Him who has created him and has given them this priceless gift, this awesome charge.

Of course just as there are many good marriages which were never solemnised in church, so there are many good parent-child relationships where there has been no baptism. By our service of baptism we do not seek to deny love and goodness wherever we find it, for all love is from God. But what we are affirming is that for Christian parents, Christ comes between the child and the parents, as indeed he must come between everything we do and have. It is this recognition which when the going gets rough – broken nights, teenage rebellion – will enable the parents to continue to give of their love, even when there has been failure on either side. Perhaps one of the hardest things to learn is to apologise to one's children. Thomas's parents will then not do God a favour in coming here with their child. They will not offer God something which he has not already got. They will acknowledge what is the true position, that God has given them their son. Like the bread and wine of communion, all things come of God. Of his own do we offer him.

Second, in expressing their act of faith by having their helpless child baptised, the parents will do all that they can do. This is a situation which we do not much like facing. We want to be in control, know that by our own efforts we can bring things to a successful conclusion. We do not like accepting that there are times when there is nothing else we can do, except watch and wait – and pray. We see this most commonly in death. What for most should be a natural process to be accomplished as peacefully as possible, becomes a frantic attempt to avoid facing reality, a pretence that it cannot really happen. So the dreaded word is avoided, the dying are given no chance to make peace with men or God. In England at any rate while doctors see it as quite natural to prepare a mother for birth and deliver her baby, few prepare their patients for death or are present at it. Yet faith by definition means that one cannot have all the answers. Its an abandonment to God, a letting go, or like Abraham a going out where one knows not. All one can do is to step forward. The faithful man is in the end the powerless man, for he has surrendered his destiny to his Father. Thomas's parents and Godparents have done that for themselves. And now they seek to do it for Thomas too, knowing that not even his faith can be assured. They will do all they can do at this moment: no more can be asked of them. They must watch and wait – and pray.

Third, the parents know that God cannot be mocked by what is done here, for it is not we who baptise but the gracious God who acts. Just as in Ezekiel's vision, God breathed new life into the dead bones of captive Israel every bit as helpless as a new-born child, so now he will breathe new life into Thomas, the life of the Spirit. This is the parents' act of faith. What they want for their son is that he will show in his life those gifts of the Spirit which are the believers to exercise through the grace of the God who so richly gives them. In every one they show themselves in different ways: but their common purpose is to bring peace – that wholeness and harmony throughout creation which can only be expressed in the poetic terms of a return to the Garden of Eden. So Isaiah looks forward to that day when the lion lies down with the lamb and children play in safety by snakes' nests, where nations beat swords into plough-shares and spears into pruning hooks. Then the kingdom for which we are bidden to pray daily will have come, come in all its fullness. We believe that in the service of baptism we take a step forward to the realisation of that day.

But just as exiled Israel had to appropriate Ezekiel's vision of new life, remain faithful to him in Babylon and so make a return from exile possible, so Thomas will have to appropriate for himself what God has done for him at his baptism. By it he becomes part of the community of resurrection, those who have passed from death to life through receiving the Spirit. In baptism we identify with Christ's death, burial and resurrection. We go down into the waters of baptism to rise into the new life of the church. We become part of his body. But to do this we must like him be prepared to stretch our arms upon the cross ready to embrace all men with his love.

For what Thomas must appropriate is not his salvation – that was won for him once and for all on Calvary – what he must appropriate is the very sign with which he will be marked, the cross itself. It is a sign which most of us have not the courage to look at for long. We take the body down, clean the demonic instrument of death, and wear it round our necks for safety. But it is the most unsafe sign in all the world. For its signifies our willingness to be torn apart, stretched beyond the limit. The Christian has no other property he may call his own but his cross, the cross which the Saviour bids him take up and follow, the cross by which he loses his life. This is the measure of our seriousness in baptising a child. This is what this boy's parents must want for him, the example which they are prepared to set him. This is what we who will receive him into our fellowship must want for ourselves. And what better day to baptise him, than Passion Sunday.

So it must be our prayer, as it will be his parents and Godparents' prayer in the years ahead, that Thomas will confirm our faith by proclaiming his own faith, and will with us kneel to receive the body and blood of his Saviour who empowers us to go out from this service to bind up the broken-hearted, to make whole what has been shattered, to free all who are enslaved, to proclaim the good news that God has in Christ visited and redeemed his people. But others will only take our message seriously in so far as they see in us those who understand the true cost of discipleship, that grace can never be cheap, that we have indeed taken up our cross and followed the Saviour in making his passion our own.

2

ADMISSION OF SCHOLARS

For the last eight years, I have been Headmaster of the King's School, Canterbury. Early in the academic year, in a simple but moving ceremony, the Dean admits the new Scholars to the Cathedral foundation. These boys and girls can hope that eventually they will go on to hold positions of considerable influence. While there is nothing to be gained by eschewing power and the opportunities which its exercise may bring, nonetheless, the Christian will need to remember that it is in powerlessness that God is most effectively at work.

MARK 9.36–37:

> 'And he took a child, and put him in the midst of them; and taking him in his arms, he said to them, "Whoever receives one such child in my name receives me; and whoever receives me, receives not me but him who sent me".'

We have just put our new scholars in our midst. I have no doubt that like the rest of the 217 new boys and girls joining our community this term, they felt nervous, even vulnerable. It must be so much easier for the Rugby players returning from their tour of Australasia, so much easier for those members of the choir who have already sung in Concert and Service in this Cathedral. They know their way to Birley's: they know the difference between Palace and P3. Yet what the Gospel tells us is that Jesus identified himself not with the secure and safe, those who know their way around, but with a nervous child being gaped at by all.

Mark places the disciples' discussion on who was the greatest in the context of Jesus's second prediction of his Passion. The Son of Man will be delivered into the hands of men, and they will kill him. Jesus's life is moving to its climax, death on the cross as a common criminal at the hands of the occupying power to whom he will be delivered by his own people. He had spelt it all out to the disciples; but they did not understand his saying, and they were afraid to ask him.

Like so many of us they were afraid of facing reality. Of course, they ought to have known that it could only end like this. They were no strangers to suffering – no strangers to the knowledge that God's purposes are achieved not by power, but by powerlessness. Were they not in origin escaped slaves? Had not Moses had to die on the far side of Jordan in order that his people could enter the Promised Land? Did not the exiles in Babylon like a second Moses have to die in a heathen country in order that their children might once again possess their land? But contemporary Judaism longed for a triumphant Messiah, longed for a deliverer from the cruel Romans, longed that Israel might once more be a political power. So the disciples refused to face facts and instead debated who was the greatest.

But God does not work through principalities and powers: they are ranged against him. He entrusts his future to a baby floating in a basket in the Nile; to a baby lying in a manger in a backyard of an inn. God can only be God in naked vulnerability.

So Jesus sets a child in their midst. He does not choose a child for innocence: children are not innocent. He does not choose a child for silence: children are not silent. He chooses a child because children are dependent, vulnerable, at the mercy of adults. Like the Son of Man, they have no status: like him they suffer rejection, abuse, torture and death – even in our own so-called civilised society.

Christian discipleship, if it is to be true, cannot be about rank, office, hierarchy: it is about service – being without status, at the mercy of one's masters. Of course, all too often, Christians like the disciples of old have sought to avoid this ugly fact. From the time of Constantine, they have sought to master rather than be mastered; like the worldly they are terrified of being dependent, vulnerable, powerless. Like the worldly they court success, debate who will be greatest.

Those who are prepared to become like children will always be a minority – but it is with the powerless that God makes himself known, achieves his work. For it is only in our nakedness that God can truly be God within us – when we have nothing to rely on and stand before him in our utter dependence – then he can clothe us as he clothed the first man and woman in the Garden. We don't have to be innocent. God is not put off by our shame: it is our efforts at self-protection that keep him out, make any talk of faith redundant.

But worst of all, Christian preachers have all too often chosen to twist our Lord's injunction to become like children. It threatens their structures, their security, their power: instead of embracing powerlessness, they have enjoined meekness, subservience and built the Saviour in their image – gentle Jesus, meek and mild.

But no reading of the Gospels could support such perversion. The prophet from Nazareth is assertive, angry, even violent in the cause of the Kingdom. He attacks the Jewish authorities, throws the money-changers out of the temple. Nor is He tempted to restrict that anger to his fellow men. Like the patriarch Jacob, Jesus wrestles with God in Gethsemane; like the unjustly suffering Job, cries in anger at God on Golgotha – my God, my God, why hast Thou forsaken me? There is nothing meek or mild in that final onslaught on the God who refuses to answer, and allows Jesus to suffer that ultimate act of powerlessness, which we all must suffer – death itself.

If, then, the cost of discipleship means embracing a naked vulnerability, it need not be lived out in silence. It is the guilty disciples who have been discussing power who remain silent at Jesus's questioning. As parents and teachers know, no word is more frequent on a child's lips than 'why?'. It is also the essential ingredient of all scholarship. And that 'why' is to challenge not only the principalities and powers of this world, but God himself.

And for the disciple called to follow by his master, that challenge must echo from the very cross he enjoins him to take up. For it is only there that stripped of all protection and pretension, the disciple is made most fully vulnerable, only there that his outstretched arms can embrace total powerlessness.

Amid all our anxious efforts to ensure the security of tomorrow, few have grasped the Gospel's essential radical-ness. But it is those few who herald the coming Kingdom – a Kingdom characterised not by the disciples' discussion on who shall be greatest, who will have most power, but by a powerless child standing vulnerable in their midst.

3
THE SERVANT
Symbol of Divine Powerlessness

Once a year in Hertford College Chapel, Oxford, the Macbride sermon is preached. While in multi-faith Britain the intention of its founder – to combat Jewish theology and convert its adherents – can no longer be accepted at face value, nonetheless Macbride gives the preacher the chance to examine Hebrew texts and relate them to the Messianic claims for Jesus. None has been more important for Christian interpretation than the famous prophecy of the suffering servant of Isaiah 53.

PRINCIPAL Macbride has laid down that the sermon which commemorates his name shall be preached upon the application of the prophecies in Holy Scripture respecting the Messiah to our Lord and Saviour Jesus Christ, with an especial view to confute the arguments of Jewish commentators and to promote the conversion to Christianity of the ancient people of God. One cannot but envy such an expression of confidence so out of tune with our own times. It was something of a relief to find in the Vice-Chancellor's invitation the sentence that recent preachers of this sermon have allowed themselves some latitude in interpreting Principal Macbride's request. I hope I will not be thought perverse when I say that I shall by and large concentrate on one text which Principal Macbride would have thought messianic, though that text was not so interpreted by Judaism of our Lord's day, nor, as recent scholarship has shown, did it acquire much Christian importance until patristic times. I refer of course to the great suffering servant poem, Isaiah 53.

But before I can talk about the poem itself, it is necessary to sketch an outline of its author's theology as found in Isaiah 40–55.

Nothing is known of the anonymous prophet though there seems no good reason for doubting that the event which sparked off his work was the appearance in the east of the all conquering Persian prince, Cyrus, whose victories were even now threatening Babylon. If we may then with some confidence date the work to the latter part of the exile, everything else about it remains uncertain, even its place of composition. For while traditionally the prophet has been thought of as writing among his fellow Jewish exiles in Babylon, there are also good arguments for a Jerusalem origin. For there is no doubt that the prophet is intimately concerned with the holy city which as he proclaims at the start of his work has suffered double for all her sins. His hope is of a renewed Jerusalem to which the faithful will return from all four points of the compass to which they had been dispersed and from which God's *torah* and *mishpat*, his law and justice, would go out to the ends of the earth. But wherever the prophet was writing, it is clear that the event which is to inaugurate the process of restoration is the return of the Babylonian exiles in what is deliberately pictured as a second exodus. Israel's destiny lies with them for without their continued faithfulness against all the odds any future, let alone the amazing events which the prophet heralds, cannot be realized.

The prophet makes his appeal not merely to an Israel weary of exile, but to an Israel whose fathers had themselves been promised deliverance and restoration. But the return from exile prophesied by Ezekiel had not taken place. Fathers had died and sons found themselves still in Babylon in an exile for which they themselves were not responsible and about which God seemed at best indifferent, at worst impotent. Against all reason both in Palestine and Babylon there were those who had remained faithful to God, relying on another act of divine grace to bring about their deliverance.

As they watched their contemporaries dying in heathen Babylon, they naturally questioned whether such loyalty had been misplaced. Perhaps after all God had finally rejected Israel. This was the logical conclusion of Deuteronomic covenant theology, even if the Deuteronomists in expressing hope for the future argued against the full implications of that logic. Perhaps Ezekiel had been a false prophet bringing hope where there was no cause for hope. Perhaps the Babylonian gods were stronger than Israel's God, and he had been defeated. What was undeniable to the new generations of Israelites in capitivity and in Palestine was that in spite of faithfulness in affliction, God appeared totally inactive. It is against this background that the prophet proclaims his message. His task is to answer the people's question: what, if anything, is God doing? The answer is clear. Even now, if only they have eyes to see, God is bringing about their salvation – an event of such colossal proportions that it will eclipse even that salvation event which originally brought Israel into being. So it was no accident that this Persian prince, Cyrus, had appeared in the east. It was all part of the divine plan. Indeed, Israel's release is not just looked forward to as an event in the future, it is even now breaking in, being realized. And it will take the form of another exodus in which nature will once more be transformed as at the Red Sea, but which this time will not be a night-time dash for freedom, but a measured triumphal march across a transformed desert in the sight of all the nations. And throughout the journey God will guide and protect the returning exiles from every peril over which they might have anxiety. Further, God's deliverance of his people is now so imminent that the prophet can actually command the exiles to depart at once.

But while this second exodus is pictured as on a far grander scale than its predecessor, it is not to be thought of as a mere re-enactment of history. It not only far surpasses its predecessor, it obliterates its memory. For Israel is commanded to remember it no more (Isaiah 43.16–21). But that the event which had inaugurated Israel as the people of God should now be dismissed from national consciousness is nothing less than blasphemy. Yet throughout the prophet's work it is the new action which God is now taking which is stressed. The reason for this is that the prophet sees the forthcoming return from exile not as a straightforward continuation of Israel's history, but as an entirely new start. All exilic and post-exilic theology stresses the radical discontinuity between Israel before the exile and the restored people. So while the prophet freely draws on exodus imagery, nowhere does he refer to the covenant made at Sinai. For Israel's future does not depend on her obedience to the law there inaugurated, but simply on her election which has been willed by him who is God alone, who has created all things, and whose gracious action will be witnessed by the nations to the ends of the earth. It is then no surprise that while omitting the Sinai covenant, the prophet none the less draws on the other three Old Testament covenants – all covenants of sheer grace – those with Noah (Isaiah 54.9ff), Abraham (Isaiah 51.2) and David (Isaiah 55.3). For the use of these covenants confirms *both* the everlasting *and* unconditional nature of God's future relationship with his restored people, which is summed up in the prophet's transfer of the promise to David to the people themselves:

> Come to me and listen to my words,
> hear me, and you shall have life:
> I will make a covenant with you, this time for
>   ever,
>   to love you faithfully as I loved David.

This radical treatment of the Davidic covenant indicates that the prophet saw no significance in a future Davidic king. For him, the return from exile was not to be inaugurated by any messianic figure. It would be the restored community of Israel who would witness the saving power of God to the world (Isaiah 55.5).

Yet for all the assurances which the prophet lavishes on his hearers, he himself remains anxious about the outcome. It is by no means certain, and God is himself powerless to assure it. If the exiles as a whole apostasize, then there will be no second exodus, no event whereby the general restoration of the dispersed can take place and God's *torah* and *mishpat* brought to the nations. The prophet is painfully aware that it is not only Israel's future that is in the balance, but God's too. And the prophet knows that the cards are stacked against him. Indeed the prophet's own work illustrates the necessity to combat the claims of Babylonian religion. While the exiles' deliverance may be at hand, until that deliverance is recognized as a fact, they must continue to live by faith. There is no other way. A destiny far beyond their wildest dreams awaits them – far more than a mere Deuteronomic re-entry into the land – for they are to be the catalysts of the new Israel which will inaugurate God's rule of justice and peace throughout his world even to the farthest places.

But if a second exodus which entirely surpasses the exodus from Egypt, indeed which eradicates it from the historical consciousness of Israel, is to herald Israel's restoration, then one would expect this to be headed by a second Moses who would himself surpass his prototype of the Sinai desert in the amazing nature of his ministry. This new Moses I believe to be the model for the prophet's suffering servant of the four servant songs, for Moses alone of all Israel's heroes was specifically said to have suffered vicariously at God's behest. So Exodus 32 describes how Moses, following the incident of the golden calf, sets out to make atonement for Israel by offering his life for his people's sin. God rejects his offer, confirms Moses in his task of leading his people to the promised land, and issues an ominous threat of punishment at some undetermined time in the future. The Deuteronomists inherited this tradition, and writing in the light of the implementation of that threat, used it to explain why Moses did not enter the promised land, but died in sight of it on Mount Nebo. So three times in the introduction to the book of Deuteronomy (1.37; 3.26ff; 4.21), they record that God refused Moses entry into Canaan demanding his death in Transjordan for the rebellion of Israel in the desert. Instead of leading his people triumphantly across the Jordan, Moses is instructed to look across the river at the full extent of the promised land and so take possession of it on Israel's behalf, for this was the recognized legal way by which the conveyance of land was effected. Although innocent of any offence Moses must die vicariously for his people's sins.

But establishing the model for the suffering servant does not mean that we have discovered that servant's identity. Who is to be the new Moses of the new exodus? The answer must surely be those who against all the odds are prepared to remain faithful and so make possible that new exodus. And this is confirmed from the second servant song where the servant is identified as Israel (Isaiah 49.3), but only two verses later pictured as having a mission to Israel (Isaiah 49.5). In other words the servant is that righteous remnant which does not apostasize but which in the face of the apparent inactivity of God is still prepared to hang on and trust him and so secure the future of all Israel. So it seems to me that we are to see in the dying generation of the faithful exiles a direct parallel to Moses who like them had to die in a heathen land beyond the Jordan in order that his people might enter the promised land. And their faithfulness in suffering would ultimately have a world wide significance. Indeed, it would no longer be the Moses of the first exodus who was remembered, but the faithful few in Babylon who made possible the second and so the return to Jerusalem of all the people of God wherever he had scattered them.

But the servant's role does not stop with the re-establishment of Jerusalem and the return of the dispersed. As the first servant song makes plain, his vocation is to bring forth *mishpat* throughout the earth (Isaiah 42.4). This word is usually rendered in English by judgment or justice. But it really stands for applied law – actual decisions of the courts. And since such legal decisions were held to reflect, like all Israelite law, God's will, then to bring forth *mishpat* means in effect to apply God's will to the whole stratum of life: in other words to establish that reign of justice and order to which earlier prophets had called Israel and which is reflected in those messianic poems Isaiah 9 and 11 to which Principal Macbride would draw our attention.

So the second song not only confirms a faltering servant in his task of restoring Israel but reminds him of his greater responsibility to be a light to the nations (Isaiah 49.6). But the one role leads on to the other for as a result of the miraculous deliverance of the exiles and the return to Jerusalem the leaders of the foreign nations will feel compelled to come and prostrate themselves before Israel in Zion, and thereby submit to God's authority (Isaiah 49.22f). So the servant will fulfil his commission as a light to the nations whose own representatives will take to the farthest places of the earth God's *torah* and *mishpat*.

In those prophecies that form the final section of the canonical book of Isaiah, Isaiah 56–66, this same picture of Israel as the mediator of God's rule to the world is preserved. For in Isaiah 61.5–7 modelled directly on the first servant song, while the nations are described as the laity in ancient Israel supplying the non-property-owning priests with the material necessities of life, Israel is seen as their priest, one of whose duties was to teach Yahweh's *torah*. Thus this later prophecy pictures the fulfilment of the servant's commission in the first song with Israel establishing throughout the world the practice of the complete will of God, his *mishpat*. The importance of the vision of Isaiah 61 is that it confirms that in the new age Israel is not destined for political superiority to be maintained by force of arms, but rather is to be the servant of the servants of God maintaining world peace through the dissemination of his *torah* and *mishpat*. Israel, now no longer a nation but a worshipping community, is thus at last able to fulfil her original call

given her at Sinai to be a kingdom of priests (Exodus 19.6) –
a role which her long period of nationhood had paradoxically prevented her from realizing.

And of course *shalom*, peace, perfect order and harmony
is the inevitable result of the acceptance of God's *torah* and
mishpat, as the probably exilic poem in Isaiah 2.2–4, re-
peated in Micah 4.1–4, affirms. There the nations come to
Zion for general instruction in God's *torah*, just as long
before Israel had gone to the mountain of the Lord, Sinai,
for a similar comprehensive body of teaching. And since the
nations now subject themselves to God's law, war becomes
an impossibility. Law thus achieves its avowed aim of
ensuring perfect order. Weapons of war can be forged into
agricultural instruments as each man cultivates his land in
the knowledge that eternal peace reigns over all mankind.
Jerusalem thus becomes the centre of a transformed world
no longer concerned for power and domination, but only
that God's will might prevail. Here we see her fulfilling her
role as priest to the world.

But the promise of this oracle depends solely on the grace
of God. It is not man's to achieve but results from the prior
action of God in establishing the primacy of Mount Zion
just as the new exodus from Babylon depended on his grace
alone. The coming of the kingdom depends then entirely on
divine initiative. Israel of herself cannot inaugurate it. But
the possibility of such an inauguration will depend on there
being a faithful mediator, a new Moses, who will be available on the appointed day to act as God's servant. Israel's
part is to provide that continuity of faith without which
God cannot bring about the final reign of peace. But the gift
of that reign and the time of its dawning depends entirely
on God, and on God alone.

But how is the servant to achieve his task? The third and
fourth servant songs make this plain – by suffering. There is
no other way. And in the third song, Isaiah 50.4–9, the
servant consciously accepts it as part of his ministry. But it
still remains to spell out the full nature of that suffering.

This comes in the fourth song, Isaiah 52.13–53.12, which begins with the exaltation of the servant. It is clear that he has fulfilled his ministry for he is acknowledged by the nations and their kings. Further he has fulfilled it not by using force, but by allowing the ultimate in violence to be done to him. Utter horror is expressed over the servant's bestial state and total astonishment at the utterly unbelievable turn of events which his exaltation brings. Clearly this is something without any precedent – the prophet's new thing.

There then follows a confession by those who ought to have known better – apostate and indifferent Israel. The servant's sufferings are described at considerable length, though since this is done through poetic imagery, a number of different motifs being used, we are prevented from carrying out any precise analysis as to what was involved. But it is clear that the poet is intent on stressing that the servant was spared no degradation whatsoever. And further this suffering was continuous from the moment of birth to death itself – an exact parallel with those faithful and innocent exiles to whom the prophet was appealing to remain faithful.

The servant voluntarily accepts his role as vicarious sufferer. This involves not merely sickness, abuse and assault, but even death. And he is buried as an outcast of the community. Again the poet gives no precise indication as to how the servant died. His intention is simply to assert his death and burial for this is the ultimate destination of his mission. He is not merely to endure sufferings: he is to be annihilated through them. Only beyond death will he secure his vindication.

But the servant's exaltation should not be understood in terms of resurrection for this doctrine was not yet part of Jewish theology. The poet relies on conventional psalmic language. Yet it is clear that the servant's vindication can be seen in his offspring. His death does not lead to his extinction. There will be a future. Yet it is to be understood as an entirely new beginning for it arises beyond the grave. The servant's death marks the end of the old order: through that death a new start is made, a new relationship between God and Israel is achieved, which ultimately involves all nations. But it can only be achieved by the servant suffering his own apparent annihilation.

Clearly the prophet's intention is to assure the faithful exiles that if despite their faithfulness they must die in Babylon, nonetheless their endurance will secure a future for their children, indeed for all men, beyond their graves in a heathen land. This explains why the suffering and death of the servant are still pictured as in the future, as in his vindication. It is the prophet's task to make him understand the mission for which he has been designated. Unless he does this, there can be no future for Israel, for the world. The situation is desperate and demands immediate response. Thus the servant is no messianic figure of the future: he is anyone who will continue faithful even though he may never himself experience the imminent restoration of his people. Contrary to appearances the future depends not on God, but on the exiles themselves.

Isaiah 53 plays very little importance in the rest of the Old Testament, Apocrypha and Pseudepigrapha. Further, within the Christian canonical and extra-canonical literature it is only used either as a proof text showing that the details of Christ's life did fulfil Old Testament prediction or for encouraging humility. Why was the servant ignored?

Although the Persians permitted the exiles to return to Jerusalem, the elect community remained a small and insignificant religious movement which turned in on itself to preserve itself. Thus the prophet's vision of the world-wide acknowledgement of God's *torah* and *mishpat* was not fulfilled. And with the advent of the Seleucids under Antiochus Epiphanes, not for the last time, the very existence of Judaism was threatened by direct extermination. It seemed now that the historical process of salvation history was at an end and that the only hope for the future lay with God bringing history to an end and inaugurating the final age. Hence the rise of apocalyptic and the birth of the son of man of Daniel.

And while Jesus never rejected acknowledgement of himself as messiah, it is clear that he deliberately clothed his messiahship in the image of that son of man. In Daniel this figure is identified with the saints most high, that is those faithful Israelites who are enduring persecution but who will be vindicated. What Jesus does is to take this plural concept of the son of man and apply it to himself alone. He is *the* son of man. His authority is being rejected; although messiah, and contrary to current Jewish teaching, he must suffer even unto death. But he will rise from the dead and all nations will acknowledge his sovereignty.

The servant was then never as such an independent concept like messiah and son of man. The songs were part and parcel of the prophet's total message – a summons to the faithful in exile to hang on so that the new exodus even now dawning might become a reality. The question who is the servant is in fact the wrong question because the author never set out to describe a particular person, but using Moses as a model to spell out the vocation of the faithful people of God.

As hope in an early parousia gave way to an institutional church, the necessity to explain the work of Christ through new images grew. In retrospect, the servant seems so obvious that countless commentators have credited Jesus with this innovation, whereas it seems he worked with the current apocalyptic concept of the son of man. But he had died for all men, even those at the farthest ends of the earth, died the one true servant of God despised and rejected by those who ought to have known better. But he had also been exalted, and increasingly acknowledged, and even now his kingdom was breaking in for all who had eyes to see.

We have then cause to thank the fathers for rescuing Isaiah 53 from its Jewish/Christian neglect. It is a hard prophecy and one which post-Constantinian Christianity as well as Zionism has sought to avoid. For it speaks against the national and political, not seeking to dominate other nations or deprive them of freedom, but merely to bring them *torah* and *mishpat* – God's will for his world.

In identifying the Jewish suffering servant with the Christ on the Cross, the fathers confirmed the validity of the prophet's message and made the Christian symbol not the empty cross of the resurrected – but the cross on which hangs the bestial figure of the man who allowed himself to be annihilated – and who called his followers to the same fate. Yet for our own safety we take the body and bury it: it is easier to think of heaven hereafter, than the cost of discipleship here and now. And where bravely the figure is left, like the stall at Bethlehem, it is profaned by its romantic respectability so that we can look at it without passion. But while the servant has through his passion assured the coming of the kingdom, its realization depends on his servants whose task remains to bring to the world God's *torah* and *mishpat* that swords may be turned into ploughshares.

So through the work of the fathers the word of God which never returns empty remains valid and the identification of the suffering messiah with the servant confirms that the kingdom of peace can only be realized through the steadfastness of the faithful remnant prepared to suffer even annihilation without seeing their work realized, in order that others may enjoy its fruits. Without this vision, without the continued prayer, thy kingdom come, and without those who are prepared to effect its coming, there can be no hope for man. But to look for any other way than the way of suffering is to mistake the very nature of the God whom we seek to serve. In giving us this opportunity to remember the suffering messiah who became identified with the servant, Principal Macbride has served us well. For in the figure of the servant we see that contrary to so much that we have been taught, contrary to so much of our behaviour as

Christians, the essential characteristic of God is his power-lessness. It is that powerlessness which the Church must embrace if God's *torah* and *mishpat* is to reach to the farthest places.

4
THE GOOD SHEPHERD

I served my title as a curate at the Good Shepherd at Cambridge. It was a new church in a large and growing housing estate which in my time was only partly completed. There was no organ, bells or pulpit and the services, without losing a proper sense of dignity, had a refreshing informality about them, particularly as regards to young children. The parish was in effect a mission church – and mission always involves risk. This sermon was preached on the feast of the Good Shepherd.

LUKE 15.1–10, from today's Gospel:

> 'What man of you, having a hundred sheep, if he has lost one of them, does not leave the ninety-nine in the wilderness, and go after the one which is lost, until he finds it?'

Now I hope that you have already noted the all important element in the story. The ninety-nine sheep are not left in the safety of the fold, but in the wilderness. In other words the shepherd's act is a reckless one. Whereas you might have expected him to round up the flock and make them secure, he does the opposite. He risks the ninety-nine and goes off in search of the one. There is not time to pen in all the flock if there is to be a chance of finding the stray alive. But who knows whether robbers might not carry off the ninety-nine in his absence, or animals decimate them? Perhaps the shepherd would have been wiser to have cut his losses – after all they were only one per cent – not a bad success rate. But the shepherd out of immediate compassion for the one who has strayed risks his all. He could at the end of the day find himself with nothing.

This practical illustration from the dilemma of ordinary everyday life is used by Jesus to point to the way in which God acts. He is like the reckless shepherd who simply will not let the stray go but will risk all in an attempt to find the stray. God, says Jesus, is perpetually on the lookout for the outsider, the outcast and the lost ... the sheep who has nibbled himself into such an impossible position that his sole hope of survival depends on being found by the shepherd. It is God's concern that he should be found. He is never content with a ninety-nine per cent success rate. He knows only perfection. It is this seeking by God for those outside his flock that is the characteristic message of the New Testament. This is the gospel – the good news. No matter how far you have nibbled yourself away from the image of that nice fluffy white lamb into the stinking matted dung ridden sheep that is you, God risks all to rescue you.

This was a lesson which Israel had failed to learn. Initially anyone could have joined the desert tribes who at Mount Sinai entered into the covenant with God and thereby became his flock. With entry into the promised land of Canaan, all sorts of different peoples became part of Israel, and under King David the worship of the Israelite God became the national religion. The flock had found their fold.

But what of the foreign nations? Were they of no concern to God? It was not until the time of Israel's exile in Babylon 450 years after David that the Jews came to recognize that the other nations of the world were also part of God's creation. But because after her return from exile, Israel found herself part of a powerful heathen empire in which a great variety of gods were worshipped, she had to ensure the purity of her religion. It was therefore decreed that only those who acknowledged her law could be members of

Israel, within God's flock: the rest, the Gentiles, were excluded. Increasingly Judaism turned in on itself becoming a protection society. Converts were the exception. And by the time of Jesus it was not just the Gentiles who were excluded from Israel's religious life, but whole sections of the Jewish community itself – the tax gatherers and sinners of the New Testament – those who co-operated with the occupying Romans or had committed heinous sins.

But Jesus the Good Shepherd by continually courting the company of such outsiders demonstrated that far from being exiled from God's love, they were the immediate objects of his concern. They were sheep without a shepherd and he would risk all in recovering them. And so he did as his Son snuffed it on that bloody cross.

Jesus sums up his story: 'There will be more joy in heaven over one sinner who repents than over ninety-nine righteous persons who need no repentance'. It is the rescued sheep who understands the nature of our God – that we are only saved not by any action on our part but solely through divine grace. He comes for us, not to condemn us but with arms stretched out on that instrument of torture, stretched out to embrace not just lost Jews but all whom his Father had created and whom he willed and wills to be his own. The only question is whether they will appropriate what is already theirs.

As we read this story we can identify with the rescued sheep and take comfort from it. It is easier sometimes to see ourselves as dirty and stupid and in need of a hug. But actually of course by coming here this morning we have already identified ourselves with the ninety-nine. And we think of the ninety-nine as left in safety, forgetting that they too were part of the risk process, that they were left in the wilderness. And when we do feel threatened, we put up fences, pen ourselves in, huddle together against all threats both real and imaginery. Such is the Church in many places – a protection society cut off from the world whom her crucified Lord willed to embrace. And can it then be a surprise that when she seeks to find him in her midst, she finds him as he must always be on the hillside rescuing and reclaiming all who are his.

And if he did appear back this morning triumphantly bearing on his shoulder the dirty, smelly occupant of a cardboard box in the Charing Cross Road, if he put down here the dying victim of Aids, if he collapsed amid us exhausted under the weight of a vomitting lager lout would you share with them in the Eucharist cup, the cup of joy and rejoicing, or would you continue to huddle together for safety?

'But I mighty catch . . .' Yes you might. The Gospel is about risk. It is about risking all you have got, even your life. The journey to which those extended arms nailed in powerlessness to the wood invites you, is the journey not of self-protection, but of self-destruction. That journey may begin in the safety of this building, but its end lies elsewhere in the grime, filth and foolishness that makes up so much of life for both rich and poor alike. It is a journey to which we are all invited for paradoxically we who know that grace alone has saved us, know too that as part of the body of the crucified, we too must become the Good Shepherd and make his recklessness our own. 'What manner of man having . . . does not leave . . . and go after . . . until he finds it?' Jesus assumes that such recklessness should be the norm.

5

MINISTRY

(i) A First Mass

There is no more emotional moment in a priest's life than that when that priest first celebrates the Eucharist. It marks the culmination of all the preparation for priesthood and enables the person at last to be whom he or she has been called to be – the enabler of God's grace. This sermon was preached at the first mass of a former Oxford pupil.

I AM not all together certain to whom the sermon should be addressed. Should I talk to Adrian, give him advice and encouragement for the future? Should it be to his Vicar whom I must anyway thank for letting me preach this morning. Should I ask him to continue to care for Adrian? Or should it be to you – should I be telling you your duties to your new priest? In fact I want to talk to all of us (including myself) about priesthood.

You may be saying to yourself, that's a funny thing to do. What has that to do with me. I am not a priest. No you are not. There is a difference now between you and Adrian, and one which I would in no way wish to diminish. Through no merit of his own, he has received the grace of orders which this morning he will begin to exercise. But though he now has a distinctive ministry, we all share in a common ministry, the priesthood of all believers. What is true of Adrian as a priest is true of you too in the ministry which through your baptism, and again through no merit of your own, you have been called to exercise.

I find that I am most often asked about my call to priesthood in the most improbable places: train journies, in the pub, out to a meal – and generally by non-Christians. On reflection, perhaps this is not so surprising, for it is my experience that Christians tend to take their priests for granted, and only become interested when one of us loses our vocation, which is the polite way of saying cracks up. So my call is seen as a once for all event which guarantees that I am different from other men (as I am) and gives me a built-in protection from all future doubts and pressures (which it does not). It never seems to occur that like that other vocation, marriage, it has to be worked at daily. So when non-Christians raise the issue of my call in uncomfortably public places, the last thing I want to do is to appear pious, let alone relate that piety directly to myself. So I mumble something feeble about God, often pointing skywards with some nervous half laugh, and hope that someone will buy another round of drinks and the talk can return to the weather, or the economy or if we will win the test series.

More reflection makes me realise why Christians don't often ask me about my vocation. For Christians in attempting to express their own faith know that these things cannot easily be put into words. There is a mystery about response to God, which like the intimacies of love, is all too personal, too precious and too sacred. So at the party, in the train, propping up the bar, I hesitate to talk about my calling. It is not just that the situation might somehow soil what I have to say – far from it. It is speaking of it itself, putting it into words which in my case in their poverty, immediately make tawdry what only poetry can depict. But most of us are not poets. Yet I am sure that we must be prepared to talk about this common mystery which we have experienced, the mystery of being known and knowing God, of responding to his grace. We need to share our vocations, uncertainties and our visions – need to bear one another's burdens and so enable each of us to bear what must be born alone, the individual's response to his God. And on this day when Adrian first celebrates his priestly call, may you all through your love and prayers enable him to do that.

Strangely responding to God is a very selfish thing, for its immediate benefit is to ourselves. For what it enables us to do, whether priest or layman, before doing anything for others, is to be ourselves. Just as in my marriage, so also in my call to priesthood, I knew that without responding to that call, I could never be the person whom I had it in me to be. Of course neither by marriage, nor by priesthood, nor for that matter by a call to celibacy or the religious life, do we avoid problems: as any new convert or married man or woman knows, in responding to God we seem to acquire more of them. At the same time we find a freedom of which hitherto we could only dream: we can stand tall, fill out our clothes, for we become us.

As in all relationships, though the change is effected by the abandonment to the other, that is only the beginning. Indeed the Old Testament recognising this uses the same word of a man's relationship to God as of his relationship with his wife. And as in any love affair, there should be a steady progression of becoming, knowing as the Old Testament calls it, as love deepens and more of the beloved becomes apparent. Now we see through a glass darkly, but we are encouraged to put away childish things. Priest and layman must together venture on in the adventure of prayer and study, of care for others and self examination of oneself. The unknown is always threatening, so different from what lay behind, the certain and the concrete. But to look back is to be frozen stiff, like those photos in the family album – for only by going on can true self be found. What matters is that when at last my life and ministry near its end, I can look back and say, 'well for all the mistakes, I really am me' and even then pray for further becoming.

Our response to God in baptism and ordination does not then mean that God takes us over, frees us from decisions, risks and anxieties. We are no robots, but called to relationship. We know what that involves from our own personal lives – a succession of critical moments: letting go of our mother's womb, giving oneself to the beloved, fathering a child, bearing a child, dying – a series of risks until life is over. Its always a matter of becoming. And throughout there is a choice: right up until the moment we die as we all must die, alone and in ignorance of what lies ahead. Even then we can make a choice: we can make a good death. So it is for the priesthood of all believers: at no time are we freed from decision making, no time freed from the journey of becoming. But just as in life 'becoming' has to be worked out in the tension of human relationships, so in the Christian life, 'becoming' is worked out in the tension of the relationship with God.

And as with marriage the tensions in relationships take their toll in our joint ministry. All of us know not just from our TV screens but from our personal lives too this tension between the God of love and the inexplicable tragedies of life. To the beseeching eyes which more often in sorrow than in anger cry out: 'Why does God allow it?', if we are honest, we have no answer.

It seems a strange thing to be called to a vocation in which honesty demands silence, and profoundly unsatisfactory. But we are reminded that Jesus himself had no answer: 'My God, my God, why hast thou forsaken me?' All that he could do was to go on, on to face the inexplicable, on to allow himself to be stretched apart on the cross. Here lies the secret of all ministry. Here lies the central factor of our call. The words come cold and comfortless, and we tend to forget them: Come, take up your cross and follow me. Through no merit of our own, God has chosen us, chosen us to enjoy, not the safety of his protection, but to share in the outpouring of his divine love with which he commissions us, and brands us at our baptism, his cross. This cross must lie at the centre of our ministries so making real possibilities of which we never dared to dream. Man's hope lies not in what he himself can achieve, but solely in the cross through which God achieves in him the miracle of resurrection. So our hope as ministers lies not in our own natural skills, but in letting God make real in us the cross which he has bidden us take up and through which he wills to transform us and the world.

And it is through our baptism and admission to the sacrament of Eucharist that we become a sacramental sign of that cross seen in the eucharistic pattern of taking, giving thanks, breaking and giving. He takes us. The initiative is his. That's the mystery and the joy. No amount of preparation would ever make us fit for such a call. Like Isaiah, we have to let him claim us for himself. Our call rests not on our decision, but on his grace alone. And for all our failures, that grace goes on being given, enabling us to be whom he intended us to be. What is more he gives thanks for us, thanks for us as we are – warts and all. If he trusts us, who are we to say he is wrong?

But then we must be broken – broken not just of sin, that can never fully be in this world. No: much more fundamentally, broken of our persistence in relying on anything else but him, of our devilish pride in trying to run things our way, of trusting in our own endeavours seen most obscenely when we set out to protect God. The only way in which we can minister is as he intended us to be at our creation – naked and unashamed. It is not our faults that mask our ministry, not the humiliations which we may suffer – it is our pretences and our pretensions, our lack of honesty and trust, perhaps most of all our insistence on knowing the answers, our terror of the open-ended journey on which he has set us. So we must be broken – stretched on the wood that all self-reliance may be stripped away, so that there is nothing left but to trust him. Only then can we be given, as he would want us to be given, given as vehicles of his grace. To look for any other way than the way of the cross is to mistake the very nature of the God who claims us for his service.

But while we are all called to a sacramental expression of

ministry, the priesthood of all believers, the priest is expected to live out that expression in a peculiarly lonely and isolated manner, for it is the priest alone who administers the sacraments. Here then lies the significance of priesthood, of Adrian's priesthood. For in choosing certain people to celebrate the sacraments, and setting them apart by a sacrament itself, these people become a gracious sign of God's presence with all his people, the visible expression of his persistent love and concern that they be fed, fed with himself. Priesthood then points away from those who are called to he who calls. It guarantees no special sanctity, but rather acts as an expression of God's grace set forth in the cross. It is this special vocation that Adrian in the knowledge of his own strengths and weaknesses will now embrace both by celebrating the sacraments, and being himself the sacrament which his ordination makes him. We all pray, God bless you Adrian, in your ministry. Amen.

(ii) My Silver Jubilee

In September 1992 I celebrated my silver jubilee as a priest. The actual day fell during the Headmasters' Conference in Bruges and thanks to the kindness of the Anglican priest responsible for the Church there, I celebrated the Eucharist for my fellow Headmasters and their wives. Further celebrations followed at both the Good Shepherd, Cambridge and the King's School, Canterbury. This sermon was preached at the Parish Communion in Cambridge on the Sunday following my anniversary.

FROM the Old Testament lesson: 'And I said, "Woe is me"' (Isaiah 6.5).

From the Gospel: 'If you ask anything in my name, I will do it' (John 14.14).

Every priest acquires his own style of ministry, and there is no need to make apologies about that. Like the laity, we do not all have the same gifts: we are not cloned. What is important is that we use what we have, and that above all we use those gifts in the context of our humanity. Indeed it is my belief that contrary to so much popular understanding, all Christians have a common vocation to be more not less human, to be more what God intended in their creation. It is our failure to respond to the possibilities of being human that freezes God's world in greed, selfishness and envy.

For my part, as an Old Testament scholar, I have placed great importance on a ministry to the intellect, though I have sought to accompany that by pastoral work which extends far outside my school. But then I do not think an intellectual ministry is somehow in conflict with a pastoral one. They inform each other. Mind and heart cannot be divorced: indeed many pastoral problems result precisely from the fact that they often are. A marriage without intellectual commitment will soon founder once the emotional commitment is bruised. Indeed I am profoundly suspicious of the appeal to emotion. One knows too well how easy it is to be swept off one's feet, and the subsequent landing can be an unpleasant experience. Nor do I like gurus. I believe that all ministry should be directed at securing independence.

In an ideal world, and by that I mean heaven, ministry would be redundant. Until then both lay and ordained Christians are in the business not of counting dependents, creating a fan club, but of freeing people to be themselves. Our example remains Jesus Christ who was no guru, but came that they might have life. Having freed men and women to be themselves, he left them to get on with it.

But I would not like it to be thought that ministry was something dry and remote, a matter of books and not flesh and blood. It all depends where you locate the emotional content of religion. It will not surprise you to learn that Hebrew theology dominates my concept of ministry. Neither prophets of old nor rabbis today lack heart, and yet there is no better example of intellectual ministry. For the rabbis use their highly sophisticated intelligence to apply it to the everyday and the ordinary. It is no accident that they have become the most popular broadcasters on the early morning religious slots.

For the Hebrew mind knows that heart and head cannot be separated. Man is a whole, living unit. Without intelligence or emotion he would be less than human. But for the Hebrews intellect is found in the heart, and emotion in the pit of the stomach – the reins or bowels in the less squeamish old translation of the Bible. While the heart ensured intellectual commitment to God, steadfastness and courage, it was in the pit of the stomach that one felt what it meant to encounter his presence. And so it is whenever we encounter overwhelming beauty, supreme meaning, all that transcends our hitherto limited experience, all that leaves us spell bound and silent. There is certainly room for emotion in religion, but as the Bible from Moses to Paul illustrates, it is the emotion of awe, dread, fear – the emotion of wanting to distance oneself, the emotion that makes one feel unworthy. The paradigm remains Isaiah's vision in the temple. That vision does not encourage chuminess with the living God.

In the end we are of course all children of our age. My ministry has been exercised in a period of great liturgical change throughout the whole of Western Christianity, Catholic and Protestant alike. God has been liberated from the sanctuary, and we have been liberated from the pew as we embrace around the altar. We have rediscovered what it is to be a communion. But there is a danger that in our openness with one another, with the priest celebrating the holy mysteries in our very midst, the true emotion of Eucharist may have been lost for another, that while we clasp each other, we fail to experience the mysterious otherness of this rite – that we celebrate man and forget God.

Perhaps because I learnt my faith looking out over an ever changing and utterly unknowable sea, and practiced it in a granite church which still challenges pagan instincts never far beneath the surface, I learnt something of Isaiah's vision, learnt that without that sense of the other, the numinous, the holy, one could so easily make God in one's own image – turn Christianity into a club of people with good intentions, instead of that community called by God's grace to mirror that same wholeness, holiness that is his nature. For let there be no mistake. In baptism we are called to be the holy people – not by denying our humanity but by living at such a level of humanity that it should make others regard us with awe. Few of us achieve this in any significant measure, and we take inspiration from the Mother Teresas who do. But that does not invalidate our calling, You shall be holy: for I the Lord your God am holy.

And how are we to be holy? Here the Gospel comes in. It reminds us of what prayer must involve – we must ask in Christ's name. The name in Hebrew thought is what we would call the character. To know a person's name was to know the sort of person he was. Our prayers have to be made in accordance with the character of Jesus. His assurance of answered prayer is not an invitation to irresponsibility. Rather it is the most dreadful of all invitations, an invitation to assume the character of Christ himself.

Earlier in John's Gospel, Jesus tells his disciples they have not as yet asked anything in his name. He is not blaming them. They did not know what asking in his name would mean. It was only after the crucifixion that the truth dawned, that the invitation became a reality, that Isaiah's vision was earthed. We though have no excuse. We know what it means to ask in his name and we have before us the picture of Jesus doing just that – for was his prayer in Gethsemane not described as sweating great drops of blood? To enter into prayer in Jesus's name means to enter into the joy of pain, the victory of defeat, the life that is death. If all we care about is self-preservation, then we shall never see

Isaiah's vision of God. Looking to protect ourselves we shall be too self absorbed. But if we look away from ourselves, identify with the dirt, the stench, the bile of this divided and distracted world, then there we will find the vision of God which so often eludes us.

But to do that means not just to look on the world's sorrows: it means to make those sorrows our own. It is to have that intensity of feeling that what is theirs is ours. Then our prayers will be real. Then we shall know the pain we would be rid of, the suffering that we long to shed. Being a Christian is no spectator sport. It means joining in the game and being bloodied in it.

A priest's ministry must enable those for whom he is pastorally responsible to respond with both intellect and emotion. There must be a rigorous ministry of the word: there must also be a rigorous ministry of the sacrament. A priest who fails to stretch his congregation in the theological issues which confront them or inhibits them from experiencing the other, the numinous, dehumanizes them. For only by seeing the vision of God in majesty are we enabled to say with Isaiah: 'Here am I, send me'. Then and only then can prayer in Christ's name be answered.

(iii) The priesthood of all believers

One of the advantages of starting my ministry in a newly designated parish, was that laity and clergy recognised their essential partnership from the start. Ministry is not confined to the ordained: it is to be exercised wherever a member of Christ's body is to be found. All the baptised (lay and ordained) have a common vocation to witness to the passion of God who has marked them with his Son's cross. This sermon was preached at St George's, Paris, and was suggested by the lessons appointed for that Sunday.

THE three lessons present a rather hopeless picture of ministry: Ezekiel 2.2–5; 2 Corinthians 12.7–10; Mark 6.1–6. Ezekiel is confronted by a rebellious house, Paul is suffering under his thorn in the flesh, and Jesus is rejected by his fellow Nazarenes. If these are the rewards which God offers those whom he calls to do his will, why bother?

Ezekiel's experience of God was not a mystical revelation intended to deepen his spirituality. It summoned him to action. He is addressed in all his weakness – son of man. The expression emphasises the distance there is between God and man. On his own, Ezekiel is powerless. If Ezekiel is to do God's will, then he must rely not on his own gifts but on what God gives him. Ezekiel at the sound of God's voice had evidently thrown himself on the ground. Now God's Spirit enters him and enables him to stand before God to receive his commission. He is to be a prophet.

Prophesy is not to be confused with prediction. A prophet in ancient Israel was called by God to speak out on the contemporary issues which confronted God's people. He was much more like a leader writer of a newspaper editorial than the fortune-teller at a fete. His concern was to identify the reality of the present situation and indicate what kind of response should be made to it. Of course failure to respond as the prophet directed would lead to consequences in the future. But it was with present needs that the prophet was concerned.

God reminds Ezekiel of the nature of his people. In spite of all that God had done for them they remained a rebellious nation determined to go their own way. Ezekiel in fact experienced exile in heathen Babylon because of Israel's continued disobedience. But it is to be of no concern to Ezekiel whether his ministry is successful or not. His concern must simply be to fulfil his vocation faithfully. So it is with all Christian ministry, lay and ordained. By responding to Christ in baptism we do not enter into some business enterprise in which success is our governing motive. Indeed beware of those Christians who need to stress their success-fulness. The gospel is not about triumph, but defeat – not about winning an earthly crown, but dying a criminal on a foreign instrument of torture. The results of our ministry are not for us to determine. Our task is to be, whatever it is God wants us to be. So Ezekiel is told, 'And whether they hear or refuse to hear (for they are a rebellious house) they will know that there has been a prophet among them'. They can only know that if Ezekiel puts aside his own considera-tions and becomes what God's Spirit intends him to become. Paradoxically Christian action consists not first in doing but in being. Unless we give time for God's Spirit to allow us to be, our doing will be in our own image and not in God's – and that is idolatry. What God wills in calling Ezekiel is that his rebellious people, however they respond, should know beyond any doubt that through his prophet God had spoken to them. Vocation always provides that continuity of faith without which there can be no future for God nor man.

Paul was undoubtedly a powerful and dominating man. He had led opposition to Christianity until he had had his dramatic conversion. Then with equal enthusiasm he sought to proclaim the gospel throughout the Roman Empire. Among the first generation of Christians who had not known Christ in his earthly life, he knew he had no equal. It would have been easy for him to have relied on his own powers in presenting Christ to the Gentiles. Paul was however prevented from boasting by a serious weakness either to his constitution or personality – 'a thorn was given me in the flesh, a messenger of Satan, to harass me'. Yet although he had three times sought God to rid him of the weakness, God had refused: 'My grace is sufficient for you, for my power is made perfect in weakness.' God cannot work through those who think they are self-sufficient. He is squeezed out: no place is left for Him to operate. It is with those who know their inadequacy that God can effect his work. That is why the sinner and not the Pharisee went down from the temple more justified, why sinners and not the righteous responded to Jesus's words.

Scholars have freely speculated about the nature of Paul's affliction. It seems to me most likely to have been psychological rather than physical. It is well known that those who seek the limelight, holding audiences spellbound, often suffer from some deep insecurity. This shows itself in their private lives and results in the need for constant reassurance. Paul fits that pattern. But he had the sense to realise that the very thing he would rid himself of was literally his saving grace. We too may resent our weaknesses, but they are the stuff of humility and tolerance towards others. It is those who know their own pathetic nature in whom God's grace can most effect His will.

That Paul grasped that the essential nature of the gospel was powerlessness is shown by his insistence in his first letter to the Corinthians of knowing nothing 'except Jesus Christ and him crucified'. For Paul the cross, that moment of divine impotence, was the sole *raison d'être* for ministry. Yet Christian triumphalism has and does distort the gospel of the crucified. The power of God, that is His love, can only be recognised in His very powerlessness.

The Nazarenes could not deny Jesus's exceptional powers. His wisdom and his mighty works indicated his supreme authority. They were forced to admire his gifts and even to ask the right questions both about their origin and meaning. Where did he get all this? The answer ought to have been obvious. Both wisdom and the mighty works brought about order within the community and such order was from earliest times recognised as God's will. Indeed the Hebrew greeting shalom, peace, represents that order, harmony, all of a wholeness which is the Hebrew vision of life symbolized so beautifully in Isaiah 's vision of a lion lying down with the lamb. Jesus clearly derived his abilities from God himself.

But the Nazarenes could not face the implications of what they saw and heard. Instead they speciously denied them. Was not Jesus from quite an ordinary family up the road, son of a local trader? Were his brothers and sisters not part of the community itself? He had all the wrong background to be chosen by God for a special vocation. They dismissed the evidence of their eyes and ears and rendered ineffective any further ministry which Jesus might have effected among them. So it was to be to the end, when at the moment of greatest need he was rejected and deserted even by his disciples. Jesus did not fit the pattern of God's Messiah – how could God's reign be inaugurated by a naked figure on a cross? Jesus dies condemned as a prophet without honour.

Our three lessons then point to the essential nature of ministry. If there is to be continuity of faith, then there must be those who will embrace the vocation of expressing the very powerlessness of the God who calls them. For our God knows no other way than the way of suffering love. Ministry does not then consist in assenting to appropriate formulas of doctrinal belief: it consists in being God's suffering in his world. The community of faith is not called to express certainties, but to stand amid the doubts, tensions and ambiguities which confront all men, and in that situation

still proclaim that there is no other way than the way of
God's love. Ministry is not about selling a package – like a
brand of cereal which will make you feel good. Christianity
has nothing to do with being good. Christianity is about
passion. Ministry is recognising that one's place is not in the
city but outside it, not with one's limbs free, but pinned by
the torturers, not about covering up but exposing nakedness,
not about glory but about shame. Ministry lies not in
opening one's mouth, but in bring led dumb like a lamb to
the slaughter. Whether in the poverty of the developing
countries of the world or in the affluence of the west, the
community of faith exists as ousiders that all may be insiders.
Whatever her structures, the Church cannot be the establish-
ment for our place is with the disorientated. Her vocation is
to be despised and rejected: it must cost her her life. Security
is the death knell of faith, for there is no passion in safety.

Like the prophets of old we may well hesitate when we are
called to take up our vocation. But we are not left unaided.
'My grace is sufficient for you.' And the place where we both
receive that grace and also the confirmation of our vocation is
here in Eucharist. As our Saviour's body is broken, and his
blood spilt, so we identify ourselves with that breaking and
spilling. We do not just contemplate Christ's death; we die
with him and so share in his resurrection and ascension. As we
appropriate these mysteries for ourselves, they become ever
contemporary as we the community of the resurrection seek
to live them out by being broken and spilt, that his kingdom
may come, come in all its fullness. This is the vocation to
which he calls us. We need seek for no particular skills but
simply stretch forth our hands in faith to receive him in the
knowledge that he wills those same hands to be stretched on
the cross he wills us take up. So our blood must flow with his
blood, our body be broken with his body. This is the only way
for Christian vocation has only one symbol, the cross. It is our
vocation lay and ordained ever to represent that cross, not
safely scrubbed and cleaned, but bloodied with the Saviour
nailed upon it whose nails we proudly make our own.

6
FESTIVALS
(i) St Valentine

While Christians have their seasons for abstinence, Advent and Lent, they also have a rich variety of festivals. At Oxbridge it was customary somewhere around mid-term for the Christian community in college to celebrate an evening Eucharist and follow it by a party. St Valentine proved a popular occasion – on which this sermon was preached.

FROM the personal column of today's copy of *The Times*: 'To my little crocodile. From your big rat. All my love always.

To my sweet efficient bograt. Will love you always from the dejected Toad.

Jeremy bear loves his mouse.'

And from St John's Gospel: 'A new commandment I give to you, that you love one another; even as I have loved you, that you also love one another' (John 13.34).

Welcome to our love feast, for that is what every Eucharist is – the community of love meeting with him who is love, being embraced by him and sent out into the world to embrace all with his love. But how easily that little word love trips off the tongue. Indeed has any word been more prostituted in our time? – reduced by a mediocre media to a physical act of transitory nature. But love is the mystery of being. It was love which caused creation and which continues its expression. It is love which makes all relationships possible – love which lies at the centre of all acts of service.

Perhaps there is no greater expression of love than in a religious community, in that life of prayer and total self-offering to him who is love. If I may parody Pascal, my life is my love.

In his wisdom God has given us the luxurious gift of romantic love to learn the mystery of all love. And at the centre of such love lies both passion and paradox. Who when he first falls in love does not experience the otherness of it all, who does not feel paralysed lest anything he does should smash the mystery of the present moment. Love roots one to the ground frozen with an awesome dread. One cannot come to it by straight forward steps. It is too dazzling. There must be a courtship ritual. That's the difference between love and rape. And it is this otherness which makes today's lovers in *The Times* use animal-talk. It is a kind of protection – a way in to the awesome mystery which engulfs them, and which somehow they must reduce to manageable proportions because of the sheer magnitude of its nature. So John Osborne concludes his great play on love *Look Back in Anger*, with talk of squirrels and bears. Alison and Jimmy Porter can only come back to each other by pretending they are animals.

This evening we meet as lovers, meet with him who is love. This too is an awesome thing. Like the sacrament of animal talk, we need our aids to enable us to approach such love, the music and the mystery of our courtship ritual. For if we will only abandon ourselves to him, he will like any lover transform us into someone of whom we never dared to dream, someone who can himself love as he has never loved before. This is what is offered week by week in Eucharist. It ought to freeze one in the pews: it ought to make one much more careful of how one speaks of God, speaks to God. Most of us find it easy to think of him as imminent – readily available in our daily trivia: few of us have yet grasped the nature of his transcendence, the breadth of heaven where even angels veil themselves from the fullness of his glory.

But there comes a moment in love, when the courtship must end, when animal talk must be given up, when the lovers must see themselves stripped in their full nakedness. It can be a painful process. For while the essence of love is to accept the other as he is and not as he would like to be, one fights against such acceptance. To be entirely known is too horrific – to have no room left for privacy, pretence and prestige. But if we are to be loved, we must be loved as we are. That is the invitation which God offers. Already he has invited you to throw away your pretences as in confession you bared yourself before him. Had you the courage to be seen in the poverty of your nakedness? The mystery is that God knows it already, but we can only know the fullness of his grace as we also know the emptiness of our own condition. No wonder it is the saints who most understand the nature of sin.

Today we celebrate St Valentine. We know nothing of him – indeed it may be them, for tradition records two martyrs of that name. But the red vestments indicate that love is no dispassionate thing. It involves passion, bloody passion. The text remains true: greater love has no man than this, that a man lays down his life for his friends. It's this we want to escape from – we pass degree Christians. Not for us to be bloodied by the cross. But it is no good trying to fool ourselves about love. You cannot fall into it like a soft job, without dirtying your hands. It takes muscles and guts. And if you cannot bear the thought of messing up your homogonized faith, you had better give up the whole idea of the Christian life. For what Christ offers us in this sacrament is nothing less than the dirty business of love. As any lover knows, it will cost you your life.

(ii) Harvest

My earliest memories of worship in my Cornish village centre on the Harvest festival. The Church would groan with local produce of both land and sea. However imaginative, I have never quite felt the same excitement in similar urban worship. Tins and jars cannot substitute for the raw materials. In the country one saw the harvest gathered in and knew what a difference to local prosperity a good one made. One did not have to be told about the fragility of nature: one lived it.

HARVEST Festivals are filling country churches as at no other time of the year. The reason is not difficult to find. Harvest deals with human need. Often religion and life seem divorced from each other, and what goes on in church is of little relevance to what goes on in the rest of life. But Harvest is about survival. Despite modern technology, whether machinery or chemicals, ultimately Harvest depends on forces over which man can have no control.

Harvest Festival is then basic, earthy, crude. There is no attempt to make it appear as anything other than a direct thank you for the physical. It is about the guts of life – filling the belly. As such it evokes man's instinctive response – not sophisticated man, not intellectual man, not spiritual man, but man, ordinary human man who rich or poor depends on his food for his existence. Harvest is the most ordinary occasion: it simply acknowledges what is – that true religion is about being human. It is when the church ceases to be concerned with this essential humanity that our pews remain deservedly empty.

But, of course, in a sense feasts are always rather unreal. Everyone knows that they are out of the ordinary run of things. There is bound to be something of a bump when one comes down to earth, a hang-over when after all the fun we get back to our normal routine. Whether it is in ploughing the fields or pruning the orchards, real life is found not in the festival, but in getting on with the hum-drum, the every-day, and so making the Festival possible. Yet which of us would be without our feasts? It is these which sustain us in the ordinary – indeed which give meaning to the ordinary. All that sweat has been for this: the endurance becomes worthwhile in the joy of realisation in the feast. As a Protestant country we have a hang-up about enjoying our-selves. We somehow feel that it is not quite right, and so we have created for ourselves that contradiction of a party, the English Sunday. Happily such pharisaism is being eroded and perhaps one day we really will be Europeans and celebrate the feast of resurrection – for that is what every Sunday is – as continental Christians do.

The expression of Christian joy is a very real part of our mission to the world. But we know that we cannot leave it there. We know only too well that while life in London is good, life in Calcutta is not. We know that as we decorate our church with its festive fayre, others will know neither Festival nor fayre. The Christian who does not feel some tension as he puts the knife into the Sunday joint has lost his sensitivity.

The Hebrews well understood this tension. They recog-nised that man was not called to suffering and pain, though this might come his way: rather he was invited to leave the desert with all its deprivations, and enter the land of milk and honey, there to feast in plenty. But the Hebrews had no illusions about the horrors which life could bring – and being a primitive society their economic survival very much depended on natural phenomena. Drought or flood could ruin them.

Hebrew man could not feast while others starved. So throughout Old Testament law, constant provision is made for those in need. No one was to fall below the poverty line, not even the immigrant. Not only were the poor entitled as of right to interest free loans from their neighbour, but these loans were themselves to be cancelled if incapable of repayment. Indeed there appears to be no limit to the scope of charity demanded by Hebrew Law. It extended to sustaining travellers on their journeys, to protecting animals, and even to giving human rights to slaves. This charity was based on one essential premise, that life mattered more than possessions, that people were more important than property. Called as they were to feast in the land of plenty, the Hebrews clearly saw that all property was held in trust for the welfare of the community at large, and therefore those who had insufficient were entitled to claim from those who had enough.

The Hebrews arrived at their theology because they recognised that what God wanted of man was that he should be fully human. On the one hand he was to luxuriate in the created order which God had himself pronounced as good: on the other he was to show that same compassion as God had shown to an obscure band of oppressed slaves held captive in a foreign land. Man in his humanity was to glory in his own capacity to enjoy the goodness which God provided: at the same time he was to free from want all those who knew no such luxury.

This theology of enjoyment and charity lies at the heart of Jesus's ministry. No one revelled in life more than him. He scandalised his contemporaries who labelled him a glutton and a wine bibber. When the drink ran out at a wedding, Jesus made an even better brew, enough to drown the whole village according to John's account. At the same time, he courted the company of tarts and crooks and worried over a widow's poverty. On the one hand Jesus revelled in the carnival welcome he received as he rode into Jerusalem in triumph: on the other, totally abandoned, he gave his life as a cheap convict. Affirmation that life is for living, and compassion to enable life to be lived – these were his hallmarks. Too often Christians have emphasised the safety of denial – preaching endurance rather than enjoyment. But it is only by loving life as it should be that man becomes sufficiently sensitive to appreciate all its horrors. To affirm life is not to deny its cruelties and injustices. Rather it is to enter into battle to ensure that Christ's Kingdom does come, come in all its fullness.

Of course being human will inevitably be risky. There will be failures. David must strive in Bathsheba's arms – Peter must deny our Lord. But God does not condemn the man who fails: the adulterous couple are the parents of Israel's most glorious King, Solomon: Peter is the rock on which the church is built. It is the man who buries his talent for safety, who denies himself even the possibility of interest, who finds himself flung into the place of wailing and grinding of teeth. For to be human always involves risks: and not all risks come off. Even through no fault of one's own, one can still land on a cross. But in an age besotted by success, failure seems the ultimate catastrophy. So men play for safety – but no ideal ever had safety for a parent.

Yet there is no greater ideal than to be human – really human – to expose oneself fully to the reality of life, its joys and its sorrows, its hopes and fears, its triumphs and defeats. And this is no well intentioned humanism, for it means at the outset recognising oneself (and all others) as created by God. It can then only be achieved as Jesus, the one perfect human, showed by total dependence on God. In this life we know that sin prevents our fully realising our perfection: yet the command remains, Be ye holy, as I am holy; be ye those who bring wholeness, harmony and order, who in affirming life make life possible for all who cannot now rejoice. For as the Bible reminds us, the land of milk and honey can only be entered if man co-operates with the God who wills his entry. The Christian is not called to make a choice between God and the world. Rather he is to affirm both, and in fellowship with his creator enjoy his creation.

All this Harvest Festival teaches, and subconsciously or not, it is this which fills our churches. As we lavish our church with the riches of the harvest, satiate ourselves in the harvest supper, we do that most religious of all things; we acknowledge our dependence on Him who has created it all: we affirm our humanity. In loving life, we are made sensitive to the needs of those who cannot enjoy what is man's basic right: to share in the fruits of the promised land. We remember the poor and the hungry. So we are encouraged to works of charity not by denying but affirming, not by hating our greed but by enjoying our good fortune.

And for all her faltering the Church remains faithful to that message. For in the Eucharist we are called to express our humanity, to acknowledge our essential dependence on God for our survival. So he comes and feeds us with supremely precious food, and together we luxuriate in the banquet, a foretaste of that final banquet which we shall enjoy in heaven. But in affirming life, we become sensitive to those without – without the means to luxuriate, outside the community of love. So embraced by God himself, God who loves life so much that he gives himself for it, we go out to embrace all who are loveless and unloveable. Then our cross, the cross with which we have been marked at baptism, the sign of our love – then our cross is seen not as our sacrifice to an increasingly demanding God, but as the expression through us of the inexhaustible love of God for his world.

But those outside our community will only be willing to receive our embrace if, when the feast is over and we are back doing the hum-drum, the ploughing and the pruning, we are then prepared to be fully human. It is no use the church telling men and women that Christ is the bread of life, if it is not prepared to live itself – live not safely causing no offence, but live scandalously, live at that depth of humanity which may lead to charges of being a glutton and a wine bibber, but which at the same time makes living possible for all who are unloving and unloved.

(iii) A centenary

This sermon was preached after a painful pastoral reorganisation scheme had been carried into effect. It was a costly process for many. The centenary of one of the churches provided an opportunity not only for looking back and giving thanks but of looking forward to the adventure of the future.

Two texts for our Centenary Eucharist: From St Luke 17.32: 'Remember Lot's wife', and from Paul's first letter to the Corinthians, 11.24: 'Do this in remembrance of me'.

Today we give thanks for a hundred years of witness to the Gospel in this place. Some of the events of those years and the names associated with them are mentioned in your centenary booklet. But only the stones could tell the full story of the ministry of word and sacrament here. Some men and women have left their memorials: the majority have none. That learned men and women have knelt here we have no doubt. But they will only have formed a fraction of that continuous community of faith who have worshipped in what Dr Gray called a hundred years ago today 'little Margaret'. For them all, may God's holy name be praised.

But my first text reminds us that there is a danger in looking back. You will know the story of Lot's wife. Because of its depravity, God decides to destroy Sodom, but allows Lot, his wife and two daughters to escape. Strict orders are given them. 'Flee for your life; do not look back or stop anywhere in the valley; flee to the hills less you be consumed'. Lot's wife disobeys: she turns round and becomes a pillar of salt.

One purpose of the story was no doubt to explain some unusual geological outcrop in the Dead Sea Valley, a place noted to this day for its curious salt rock formations. But it has another purpose too. It reminds the reader that God is God and man is man. Lot's wife's glance back was no sentimental last look at her former home. It was a deliberate attempt to catch a glimpse of the transcendent God as he descended to Sodom to destroy it. She wanted to see God face to face. She wanted the reassurance that her journey was sensible – that she ought to have abandoned all in faith. But as the men of Sodom found out, no man can see God and live. Lot's wife's glance back results in her being frozen stiff.

Our looking back also has its dangers. Conscious of the difficulties of practising our faith in this present age of indifference and neglect, and faced with awful possibilities which threaten the very existence of us all, we too may look over our shoulders at that age of faith in which the foundation stone of this church was laid 100 years ago. Surely it would be possible to see the God who now seems so elusive. If only we could get back to the vision of our founders, recapture their fervour, might not we find that assurance for which we long. In fact to make such an attempt is to be frozen stiff.

I do not of course mean that we cannot derive encouragement from the past, learn from the example of those who in other ages witnessed to their faith. That is why we have saints: that is why we celebrate today. But the past cannot confirm our faith, for faith is the present response of each believer. It is his or her abandonment to a God whom in this world we cannot see face to face. Like all relationships risk is of the essence, risk that we might be wrong.

Being human, we are tempted to minimise the risk, seek for assurance, and where better to find it than in the past. We seek to avoid responsibility for our own commitment and justify it by others. But like Adam, we stand before God naked, and naked we must make our choice. Of course we rebel against our creaturely state: our necessary separa-

tion from the heavenly realm. But dust we are and to dust
we shall return. Faith has to be exercised in the isolation of
our earthly existence and in the face of the bleakness, the
blankness of death – that ultimate test of all belief. Only by
making it so could God ensure that we could have a
relationship with him. Had he allowed us to see him face to
face, we would have had no choice but to be heavenly
robots.

Yet it is always in man's nature to avoid his true condition, the expression of agnostic faith. Like Lot's wife we
want to avoid the agony and doubt of committing ourselves
to a God who continually demands abandonment of one's
security, yet himself remains hidden. It is the Church's
refusal to commit herself full bloodedly to such a journey
that freezes so much of her life and leaves her pews deservedly empty. It is to your very great credit that not without
pain you celebrate your centenary having voluntarily abandoned the security of your parent church as you venture out
into your second century uncertain of the outcome, but in
faith.

For central to both Old and New Testaments is this
voluntary abandonment of one's security in faith – self-
annihilation. So in the first act of the history of man's
salvation, Abraham responds to God's call to leave Haran
and abandons himself in faith, not knowing where he was
to go. Such voluntary abandonment is to be the pattern for
all men and women of faith. It is a pattern which they are
called to repeat again and again. So in God's own time
Abraham is again brought to the test by the command to lift
the sacrificial knife over his son Isaac, the child of promise.
By such faithful abandonment to all that he held most dear,
Abraham showed that at no time does God's promise of
salvation become automatic. Faith has continually to be
lived out, continually reiterated through suffering and even
death. While the future always depends on God's grace, that
grace can only find expression through men of faith being
prepared to act in faith when they no longer have any cause

to do so. That this is the true human condition is confirmed when in that final act of the history of man's salvation, Jesus dies, as we all must die, alone and in ignorance: yet in the face of a God who remains hidden, expresses his agnostic faith: My God, my God why hast thou forsaken me? This is what he means by commanding us to take up our cross, and follow.

But though we cannot see God face to face, we cannot have proof that he is, we can still know him. Of course it is by faith that we do so, but he has provided the means: 'Do this in remembrance of me'. By remembering, Jesus the Jew did not mean that we were simply to take part in a memorial service for a hero long since dead. For the Jew to remember meant reactivate the event so that one experienced it for oneself, appropriated it, made it one's own. There is a Rabbinic saying of the 2nd century AD which reads: 'It is the duty of every generation to think of itself as if it had personally come out of Egypt'. Every Jew was therefore to see himself as physically taking part in that divine deliverance. So too with the Eucharist.

As the Saviour's body is broken, and his blood spilt, so we identify ourself with that breaking and spilling. We do not just contemplate Christ's death, we die with him and so share in his resurrection and ascension. As we appropriate these mysteries for ourselves, they become ever contemporary as we the community of the resurrection seek to live out the resurrection life by being broken and spilt, that his kingdom may come, come in all its fullness. The bread and the wine are the only assurance that he gives us. Yet if we will make them our own we will find that we need no other, that we can accept our human condition. We need not seek for assurance in the past, but in the present we may simply stretch forth our hands in faith to receive him in the knowledge that he wills those same hands to be stretched on the cross he bids us take up. So in the end our blood will flow with his blood, our body be broken with his body. The question which each of us individually in every generation has to answer is: Have I the courage to believe in my own salvation? If I have, then I am left with only one way of affirming my faith: do this in remembrance of me.

7
PROPHETIC VISIONS

As an Old Testament scholar, I have naturally been drawn to preach from the Hebrew scriptures. None appeal more than the prophectic books. While the earlier prophets were called to prophesy God's judgement over his people Israel for their failure to reflect his nature, later prophecy spoke of Israel's restoration and essential place in God's world – 'A light to the nations'. The following three sermons all take as their starting point prophetic texts. They are uncomfortable words – even when they express hope: for they all require response and as the word of the passionate God, that response can only be costly.

(i) Fear of self-righteousness

Two texts – one from each of the lessons. Both are words of impending doom:

> 'Thus says the Lord: "As the shepherd rescues from the mouth of the lion two legs, or a piece of an ear, so shall the people of Israel who dwell in Samaria be rescued with the corner of a couch and part of a bed".' (Amos 3.12)

> 'Then all the disciples forsook him and fled.' (Matthew 26.56)

It was the vocation of the Judaean prophet Amos to proclaim the downfall of the much richer northern kingdom of Israel. He does so in utterly uncompromising terms. Under the law, a shepherd who lost an animal in his charge was compelled to provide the owner with another animal in its place unless he could show that it had been destroyed by a wild beast. To do this he provided as evidence the indigestible left-overs, the hooves and the ears. Without such evidence, it could of course be supposed that he had disposed of the animal for his own financial gain. So Amos describes the rich city of Samaria as destined for total destruction as if a wild animal had destroyed her. All that would be left as evidence of her former existence would be the corner of a couch and part of a bed. And so it proved to be. Within years of his ministry, the Assyrians wiped the northern kingdom off the face of the map for all time.

The context of the second lesson follows on from the narration of the last supper. There Jesus had eaten with his twelve chosen disciples. At that meal he had forecast that he would be betrayed by one of them and Matthew indicates that he knows it is Judas. Now they go out from the lighted room in Jerusalem to the darkness of the Mount of Olives where Jesus tells them that in fact all of them will desert him. Peter protests but Jesus tells him that even he will deny him three times before the cock crows. To this Peter replied, 'Even if I must die with you, I will not deny you'. And Matthew notes: 'So said all the disciples'. Jesus then enters the Garden of Gethsemane to pray. Leaving the majority of the disciples together he takes his three closest friends, Peter and the two sons of Zebedee, further into the garden and tells them to watch. Returning from prayer he discovers them asleep, wakes them and chides Peter: 'So could you not watch with me one hour?' For the second time he goes away and comes back and finds them sleeping. This time he does not wake them but returns for his final prayer to the Father who remains silent. There is now no alternative but to go out and meet his fate. So Jesus returns for the last time and wakes the disciples: 'Rise let us be going; see, my betrayer is at hand'.

To understand the full enormity of the betrayal, one must remember that in the ancient near East as in the Middle

East today there is no more despicable act than to betray someone with whom one has just eaten. The psalmist in describing the depths of dereliction which a man might suffer writes:

> 'Even my bosom friend in whom I trusted,
> Who ate of my food, has lifted his heel against
> me.'

This is the enormity of Judas's betrayal but it is an enormity in which all the disciples share. What Judas hoped to gain by his action remains a matter for speculation, but the failure of the other disciples is due as all our sin is due to human weakness. Later this was to be further illustrated by Peter's three-fold denial of his friendship with Jesus. The prophet from Nazareth is utterly rejected: he goes to his death alone.

But what future is there for the disciples, broken and dejected? Their hopes lie in ruins and they know they have betrayed the one whom they loved most. Their failure could not be more complete. Yet ironically it is at the very moment of complete failure that God can be at work. For it is then that man ceases to rely on himself. So John pictures the risen Christ coming through locked doors to the fearful disciples to commission them to be his body in the world. They have not earned that commission. Indeed they have no leg to stand on. They have betrayed their Lord. Yet he will not let them go.

It is not easy to accept such unconditional love. We prefer to rely on our own ability. At best we allow God part of ourselves but reserve an area in which we may take the initiative. Indeed it is only those who have known supreme failure who can fully surrender themselves to God because they know in their shame that they have no standing: the only choice is like Judas to commit suicide or like the eleven to embrace their Lord.

But while this embrace brings great joy, it of necessity involves great cost. For it means for the disciples accepting a commission to share in the very events at which because of their betrayal they were absent. The disciples must take up Christ's cross – the cross not safely scrubbed and clean, but bloodied with the Saviour's blood whose death they must now make their own. The reason for the eucharistic meal before the night of betrayal now becomes apparent. Jesus enables the disciples through the sacrament to do that very thing. They can become his own costly love as the bread that is his body is taken, broken and given to them that they may be sent out to be Him in his divided and distracted world.

The shepherd from Tekoa faced a very different situation as he proclaimed his message at the king's sanctuary of Bethel. The people of Samaria were unconscious of any failure. Indeed the country had not known such prosperity since the days of Solomon. Riches were widely interpreted as a sign of divine blessing. Crowds thronged the sanctuaries to offer extravagant sacrifices. Everywhere there was evidence of excessive religious zeal. Yet all this was at a terrible price. For the economic boom had brought division in society. The rich had got richer and the poor remained poor. Success had become the keymark of Israelite life and it was the successful who thronged the sanctuaries. They were not in themselves bad men. Close examination of the text of Amos indicates that they saw themselves as keeping God's laws. But what they failed to recognise was that self-righteousness is no righteousness in God's eyes. They may not have broken laws; they may have done more than even the law required; but they totally ignored those who could not share in their prosperity. True the law could not lay down precise regulations concerning charity, but they ought to have recognised that it was unnatural to luxuriate while others were on the breadline. What Amos condemns is their total lack of moral judgement, their inability to perceive that being good and engaging in worship is not acceptable in God's eyes if that religion lacks any content, if it involves no cost. For the self-righteous God can do nothing. They do not need him. But what is worse, their very self-righteousness militates against the coming of his kingdom. So Amos proclaimed his dreadful judgement:

> I will punish the altars of Bethel,
> And the horns of the altar shall be cut off
>   and fall to the ground.
> I will smite the winter house with the summer
>   house;
> And the houses of ivory shall perish,
> And the great houses shall come to an end.

What then are we to deduce from our lessons? Surprisingly we find that it is in failure that God can work rather than success. It is not our sins that we should fear but our self-righteousness. Luke sums it all up in his parable of the pharisee and the tax collector worshipping in the temple. While the pharisee thanks God that he is not like other men because he has both kept the law and faithfully practised his religion, the tax collector can only stand far off, not even daring to lift his eyes to God, but merely beating his breast saying God be merciful to me a sinner. It is through such men who know the reality of their need of God's grace that his kingdom comes. The self-righteous are far too busy protecting their success, choosing to be oblivious of the needs of others while at the same time ensuring their respectability with God. But God does not care much for respectability judging by the company his Son kept. As the Bible indicates it is not the disreputable who prevent the coming of the kingdom but the reputable – those who have no need of a physician.

But we have not said the last word on betrayal – for there is an even worse betrayal which man may face – the apparent betrayal by God. Of this the psalmist knows all too well:

> 'Why dost thou stand afar off, O Lord?
> Why does thou hide thyself in times of
> trouble?'

Or – 'How long, O Lord?
       Would thou forget me for ever?
       How long wilt thou hide thy face from me?'

This was Jesus's experience. His three-fold prayer in the Garden of Gethsamene continues to be unanswered. Throughout the trial, God makes no move. No legions of angels appear. Nailed to the cross, Jesus realises that his death is inevitable.

Yet he does not resign himself to his fate: instead he argues himself towards it by hurling a question at the absent Father: 'My God, my God, why hast thou forsaken me?' There is no betrayal of God. He is still 'My God'. Rather, Jesus makes it unequivocally clear that it is God who is the betrayer. It is he who has 'forsaken' his Son. Here at the point where Jesus exhibits the reality of his humanity, at the moment of death, he also shows what is required of faith. Here is the true cost of discipleship. For death appears as God's betrayal of all that Jesus had hitherto held most dear, most of all his relationship with his Father. At the point of total destruction, Jesus has – as we shall all have to do – has to do that most illogical of all acts: express faith. Then and only then God can act. The veil of the temple is torn in two.

This then is the paradox: while despite our betrayal of Him, God still makes himself known to us: in the face of his own apparent betrayal, it is only as we express faith despite his absence that we can know his presence again.

(ii) Consequence of unrepented disobedience

Four texts from the lessons: Jeremiah 4.23–27; Isaiah 40.1–11; St Luke 4.1–13, and 22.39–53.

'I saw the earth and it was without form and
void; the heavens, and their light was gone.' (Jeremiah 4.1)

Jeremiah pictures the total desolation which is to fall upon
Israel for her failure to obey her God. That desolation will
not only involve individual suffering but the whole of creation will be destroyed. It would be as if the work carried
out by God and described in Genesis 1 had been put into
total reverse. That is the significance of the phrase 'I saw
the earth and it was without form and void'. The Hebrew
expression is *tohu wabohu*. The words picture a formless
waste – a kind of nuclear desert. The same words appear in
the second verse of the opening chapter of Genesis. This
was all that existed when God started the creation process.
From this desert God had formed his splendid creation
which Israel by her folly was now to put in jeopardy. For
the effect of sin is not only that man suffers himself but that
his whole environment suffers with him. The Hebrews had
no doubt of this. Adam's disobedience means that he can no
longer cultivate the paradisal garden but must labour against
thorns and thistles earning his bread by the sweat of his
brow. The disobedience of the generation of Noah results in
the obliteration of all life in the flood. The arrogant attempt
of the men of Babel to scale the heavens results in the
fragmentation of language so that man can no longer commu-
nicate with man.

It is not though as if God were waiting to punish man.
He has created a proper order. It is man's failure to comply
with that order which leads inevitably to judgement. That is
why it is the fool who says in his heart, there is no God. He
fails to recognise the order of God's creation and must
inevitably be the agent of chaos. Of course the Hebrews
were not so stupid as to think that bad men always got their
just desserts. The psalmists continually complain at the
good fortune of the wicked. But what they did perceive was
that that wickedness itself marred creation and rendered

impossible the order which God willed. It is not God who judges man but man who brings about his own judgement. Greed, apathy, lust for power – these are the causes of our present chaos for which God is in no way responsible. Our failure to order his creation as he willed it brings its own inevitable judgement and with it despair. For it is not oblivion that will be the result of man's disobedience, but *tohu wabohu*, a world without form and void. It is not our death in a nuclear holocaust which we should fear, but our survival.

Yet God promises through his prophet:

> 'The whole land shall be desolate, though I will
> not make an end of it.' (Jeremiah 4.27)

God cannot let his creation go. He has loved it into life and despite man's folly wills to manifest his essential nature through it. The inevitable judgement which follows sin is never the end of the story. For out of man's desolation, God wills salvation. It is this salvation to which our second lesson (Isaiah 40.1–11) referred. The prophesy of Jeremiah had been fulfilled. Israel had brought upon herself her destruction and exile in heathen Babylon. But the prophet of the exile proclaims that even now God of his own free will is preparing to bring his people home. Like the judgment, this act of grace involves not only men but nature too. The wilderness will be severed by God's road, a highway across the desert. It will be made by the transformation of nature as valleys are raised and mountains brought down, rugged places made smooth and mountain ranges become a plain. What had seemed impassable now becomes a route for God's people's triumphant march witnessed by all the heathen nations. There is no call to repentance but simply a call to appropriate faith in the nature of the God who cannot let his people go. For God does not contain within himself the will to destroy but the will to create. It is man who brings destruction, God who must be engaged in endless re-creation.

Such a God is too threatening even for the religious. They

prefer a God of judgement; a God who removes all but themselves from the sphere of his love; a God who demands man's submission before he will embrace him. But such a God is not the God of the Hebrew-Christian tradition. His love is not conditional on man's response. Of course man must accept it for himself, but it is there whether he likes to take it or not. By repenting from sin, man turns from the course of inevitable chaos to share again in God's creative process. He moves from death to life, from darkness to light. But the light has never gone out. It has continued to shine in the darkness. And it will continue to shine no matter what man may do. It can never be overwhelmed. This is the good news of the gospel.

Our lessons from the Old Testament speak to us then of a desert to be avoided, of a wasteland of our own making which will be our inevitable dwelling place unless we choose to co-operate with the God who wills us paradisal joy. But there is another kind of desert of which our third and fourth lessons speak – the desert which needs to be entered if we are to be those whom God wills us to be. So it is recorded that:

> 'Full of the Holy Spirit, Jesus returned from the Jordan and for 40 days was led by the Spirit up and down the wilderness and tempted by the devil.' (Luke 4.1–2)

It was the Spirit who willed Jesus to go out into the place of chaos, that the powers of darkness within himself could be faced. For he too had his shadow side – and if he were to be whom God willed him to be, the dark recesses had to be faced.

The temptations were real enough. They are the temptations that we all face, the temptation to be other than what God wants of us. And the subtleness of these temptations is that the action they invited was not in itself bad: it was simply not God's way. Jesus had not come to solve the material and physical problems of mankind. He had not come to establish a political empire. He had not come to force people into accepting his credentials. He had to allow the hungry to remain hungry, the powerful to exploit the weak, the continuing chaos which followed from man's refusal to accept God's way. Of course he was tempted to take a short cut, to eradicate all the misery and chaos of this world by asserting incontrovertibly his authority over it. This was the darkness within himself, the darkness to deny the very nature of himself as the embodiment of the God of love who loves despite man's rejection of Him. The temptation was not so much to force man to believe in God, but to make God's love conditional on that obedience and so of necessity to ensure it.

Without this facing of his shadow side, without this bitter experience in the desert, Jesus could not have faced the ultimate test in Gethsemane. Here was the supreme test. St Luke records his sweat was like clots of blood falling to the ground. What was at stake was whether Jesus would in fact be faithful to God's nature, would allow the hour of darkness to reign. For man's ultimate betrayal of God is about to be acted out, the killing of God's own Son. Even then things could have gone wrong. At the last moment his followers take up arms to attack those arresting him. The love of the God who will not let man go in spite of what man does could so easily have been obscured by Jesus's death in an evening brawl. This Jesus prevented. He was able to do so because he had allowed himself to be led into the desert and established the true basis for his ministry.

These two examples: of the desert which we create for ourselves, and the desert which we must enter if we are to be ourselves, provide the basis for our observance of Lent. On the one hand we are reminded that our disobedient actions will lead to inevitable chaos. We ourselves are responsible for *tohu wabohu*, not just in our own lives but in the lives of others. God continues to love us but that chaos can only be eradicated by our acceptance of his love.

Lent calls us to that task by turning and repenting of all that breaks down and destroys. But there is also a second Lenten exercise, a deliberate going out into the darkness of ourselves, a wrestling with the shadow side of our personality. Repentance of our sins may not be easy: but it only restores us to where we were before. It is the wrestling with the powers of darkness within us that lays the foundation for what we could become. While we are called in Lent to put a stop to the desert that we create, we are also called to enter the desert within. We have forty days to do so, time enough with the aid of the church's sacraments and her ministers to have the courage to do so. Then at Easter we can rise with the risen Lord to new possibilities of which we never dared to dream.

(iii) Can these bones live again?

Two texts: Ezekiel 37.3 'He said to me "Man, can these bones live again?"' and Luke 6.36 'Be compassionate as your Father is compassionate.'

The prophet Ezekiel was the first Hebrew theologian to have to come to terms with Israel's utter defeat by the Babylonians. First in Palestine and then in heathen Babylon, he had to make sense of what God had done. Gone was the temple in Jerusalem with its rituals and sacrifices: gone too were the king and leading citizens lead into exile far from their own soil. Israel was absorbed into the Babylonian empire and was to know no political independence for 400 years. As the Psalmist records, by the rivers of Babylon we sat down and wept. It was as if God had said no to any future. The colossal hopelessness of the situation is graphically described in Ezekiel's picture of Israel as dead bones lying in a desert wadi. He drew on what happened to the corpses of those killed in a bedouin skirmish: within hours the flesh was devoured by the vultures, in days the bones were bleached white by the desert sun. Nothing could have been more dead. Yet when Ezekiel is asked whether these bones can live again, he recognizes that with God all things are possible. He alone can turn death to life.

In the early part of his prophecy Ezekiel makes it perfectly plain that God had acted entirely justly. He describes step by step Israel's long history from God's deliverance of her from slavery in Egypt until his own times. At every stage Israel had been unfaithful. Long ago God ought, if he had had any sense, to have got rid of his disloyal people. But for his name's sake he had not done so. For the Hebrew's the name of a person summarized his character – and God's character was as our text from the Gospel reminds us, compassionate. He had chosen for his elect people an obscure band of runaway slaves. He had sustained them through all sorts of vicissitudes until they had entered Canaan and there established a great empire under David and Solomon. And even when that empire had through jealousy and incompetence been fragmented and largely lost, he had still preserved the rump of his people based on the sanctuary at Jerusalem where he willed to make himself known to them. But they had never understood his nature: there was only one way left to God to make it plain. He had to destroy his people, and then of his grace re-create them.

So old Israel dies. The temple is destroyed and the king deposed. Exile follows for all the leading citizens. It also follows for God for he always suffers with his people. So Ezekiel describes in the first chapter of his book how God himself leaves Jerusalem to dwell in pagan Babylon. There he wills to know again his people and from the dead bones of the old Israel to breathe into life the new Israel, an Israel who has done nothing to deserve this life but is utterly dependent on the God who wills it. The only uncertainty in Ezekiel's mind is whether the exiles will appropriate what

God offers them. Will they accept what his Spirit wills? In the opening verses of Genesis God's Spirit is likened to an eagle anxiously flapping over her nest encouraging her young to fly. It is in this anxious flapping that God's Spirit has ever since been engaged. For Ezekiel and for us, the same question must be answered: Have we the courage to be, be what God intends us to be? Will we take wing and let the Spirit make us free? Without the Spirit we can only remain dead bones.

Ezekiel's prophecy ends with a vision of God's return to Jerusalem to dwell again with his people. The final words of his book are *Yahweh shamah*, God (Yahweh) is there. They are a pun on the name Jerusalem for if you wrote out *Yahweh shamah* in Hebrew it would look very like the Hebrew word for Jerusalem. But alas history was to repeat herself and although the exiles were restored to their own land and Jerusalem and her temple were rebuilt, men still failed to understand the character of their God. Once more God had to bring about death in order that there might be life. This time though it was not to be the death of his people: it was to be his own death. Only by showing men that even if they committed the ultimate blasphemy he would still seek their re-creation, could they grasp his true nature. So outside the holy city, on a foreign instrument of torture, God died and the veil of the second temple was torn in two. The old order had ended: the dead bones were placed in the sealed grave.

Once again God re-created. The disciples saw the resurrected Christ whose new body was no longer conditioned by time and space, but went where and when he willed. And it was that new body which breathed on them his Spirit that they too might be re-created, born again, to go where and when the Spirit willed. They knew that they had done nothing to deserve this. They had indeed deserted and betrayed Jesus. They had allowed him to suffer death. But death is never God's last word. He who is creativity cannot let man go. So from the dead bones of pre-exilic Israel, a new Israel arose – so from the crucified body of the rabbi from Nazareth the church which is his body was born. Once again the disciples had for themselves to accept what God had done, and to work out the consequences of his action – that it was not just a new Israel which resulted from God's re-creative act – but a new mankind. For as St Paul reminds the Corinthians: 'we were all brought into one body by baptism, in the one Spirit, whether we are Jews or Greeks, whether slaves or freemen, and that one Holy Spirit was poured out for all of us to drink'.

In Jesus, God has then disclosed the fullness of his being. There is nothing else to say about him. We know his character in full. Nothing which man may do can put him beyond the reach of God's love. All he has to do is to accept it. He may try and run away, live as if God did not exist, but the moment he turns again towards him, he will find God not just waiting for him to tell him that he, God, was right after all, but running out to embrace him, ordering the fattened calf to be slaughtered for a feast.

It is by baptism that we accept what God offers us, that we come into the body of the church. Thereby we become the people of His Spirit in whom he wills to be his varied self. There are many ways in which we can let the Spirit show himself as Paul describes. The one body has many parts. But all those parts have one facet in common, they all bring life, for they are the work of the never ceasing creativity of the one God whose Spirit anxiously hovers that we might be, be what he has willed us to be. And that bringing of life is always achieved in one specific way, through being God's essential nature, through compassion. The compassionate grace which God has shown to us, and which unfreezes us to be, be as he intended us to be, will when we mirror it free others too. Our theology can only be liberation theology.

Much of mankind is imprisoned not by evil but by a mistaken sense of justice. But justice for God does not lie in giving man his just deserts. Justice is about dead bones. As

Hebrew law already knew long before Luke wrote his Gospel, justice is being compassionate as God himself is compassionate. It means doing good to those who hate us; offering the other cheek to our assailant; giving the thief who has taken my cloak, my shirt too; lending without hope of repayment. So often Christianity is mistakenly presented as being good. Nothing is more stultifying. Church pews are suffocated by goodness. Christianity is about being love, being reckless, abandoning oneself, risking in daft ways – ways that so often lead to one's own hurt. Respectability is not the hallmark of Christianity but scandal, the scandal epitomized by the Father running out to embrace his wanton son while the good brother complains, the scandal of the slaughter of the fatted calf.

Ironically it is because we too have opted for goodness that we need to join in the Father's feast, need to be fed by him with his very self. This is not to deny that we may not always like ourselves as we are, that we cannot be wanton. But on the whole we are not bad people, and all too often enjoy criticising those who are. What we ought to be asking ourselves is are we people of the Spirit, are we free or has respectability dulled us to his impact. In Ezekiel's words – Can these bones live again? Through God's action in this feast to which we now come, they can.

In the feast, the priest takes the bread, gives thanks for it, breaks it, and gives it to the communicants. That is what we must allow God to do with us. We must let him take us as we are, take us with our successes and our failures, our loves and hates, our respectability and what we dare not admit even to ourselves. In coming to the feast we do not have to do anything, be anybody. We have simply to come. And marvellously God gives thanks over us as we are. This is always the way of love. God does not simply accept us, he desires us, wills to embrace us in our mediocre respectability. But he does not leave us there. He breaks us, breaks us from all that stops us being him in his world, all that restrains that compassion which he wills us exercise. And then he gives us, gives us to his divided and distracted people that we might love both the unloved and unlovable. In this feast all that is made possible, as having confessed our failure to be Spirit-filled, we forget ourselves and come to the altar to be fed by him and sent out to bear him where he wills us to be. It must of necessity be a repetitive pattern as week by week we allow him to break us yet more that he might be more through us.

The exiles with Ezekiel in Babylon asked of God when he would act on their behalf. Today many ask similarly for God to show himself in action. But what is at issue is not whether God will act in our time: it is whether we will accept what he has already done, whether we will allow him to re-create our dead bones that his Spirit of compassion may be let loose in his frozen world. The priest will dismiss us by sending us out in the power of the Spirit: it is up to us whether we believe him, but if we do, we should not be surprised at anything which might happen.

8

DEATH AND REMEMBRANCE

Christians cannot have all the answers. While the New Testament hardly attempts to grapple with the problem of unjust suffering, Job remains rightly agnostic about it. Refusing to deny his innocence or abandon his belief in the just God he affirms both. Unlike the three friends, he is specifically rewarded for what he has said. Faced as we shall all be by the unfairness of life, we must neither deny it nor the God who mysteriously we find to be in it – though in this life he cannot explain the why of it.

Because of my ministry largely to young people, I have had to officiate at a number of tragic funerals. They are heartbreaking occasions and one can do little but be there and go on being there. There is no problem that can be 'solved': just a fact to be absorbed. It's a long and painful process and needs both patience and persistence – and there will always be a gap.

The following address was preached at the Memorial Service for a man suddenly cut off in mid-life. It is followed by a homily given at the school cenotaph on Remembrance Day.

(i) Freedom and Tragedy

Text: I Peter I.3–9

First, let us give thanks, thanks for Peter, for all he has meant to us. We all knew him in different ways, as husband, son, father, brother and friend. We have much to be grateful for in his love and friendship. None of what we have enjoyed with him can be taken from us.

Yet this is a cruel meeting, and God himself who knows all about cruelty, would acknowledge that. We cannot believe that Peter's death was his will, for the picture of God we receive from scripture is not of a God who destroys, but of a God who gives life; not of a God who wants sorrow, but of a God who brings joy, not of a God who cuts short, but a God who fulfils. We cannot accept that God wills our grief for Peter's early death. That good can come out of tragedy is of course true, but that can never justify the tragedy.

So if God did not will this tragedy, could he not have prevented it? Why must we suffer? But God does not control our actions. He has given us total freedom within his world to do and be what we will. The price of that freedom is that tragedy cannot be avoided. Yet would we want it other? For is not the freedom to be what we will be and to do what we will do life indeed? It is this which makes us men and not machines, which makes every day a precious experience to be enjoyed for its very self, which Peter's zest for life confirms.

No, God neither willed our tragedy nor could he have prevented it. Where was he then? He was present in it. God himself grieves with us in our grief. One of the earliest heresies which the Church Fathers rejected was that God could not suffer. But at the heart of Christianity lies passion. It is by the tragedy of his Son's death, that the Father convinces men of his true nature. God is love and his love is expressed most fully in passion.

Paradoxically our task today is to echo the writer of the letter from which I have taken my text: 'Praise be to the God and Father of Our Lord Jesus Christ.' This letter was written to a church facing persecution and addressed to the newly baptised. The author does not pretend that Christian life will be smooth, that suffering, even tragedy, cannot occur, and nor should we. But what he does affirm is that the inheritance to which we are born is one that nothing can destroy or spoil or wither. Why? Because Christians experience through their own faith that Jesus is risen from the dead: they know in their own lives the power of Christ. This does not mean that we should pretend that tragedy is not real: Jesus wept at a young death. It does not mean that God fills the gap left by Peter's death. That would be a grave insult to Peter. No the gap remains, and will remain for Peter is to be remembered, treasured, thanked and prayed for. It means though that his death is not the end of his story, that we can entrust him to the God and Father of Our Lord Jesus Christ. Death has no dominion over Peter: he is in the gentle hands of the Lord of life. He has started on a journey which we all must follow, and which as we proclaim the Easter faith we can with confidence follow.

Until then God calls us to live, live life as Peter lived, live it in all its fullness. And for Christians this will mean proclaiming within all the proper doubts, ambiguities and unhappy tragedies which confront our world, Jesus Christ is risen. As we make real our passion in the context of Christ's passion, we make real to men the possibility of a future for which so many never dare to dream. We become what the writer of our letter wills us to be – a living hope. Is that not what Peter would have wanted too? – that you and I should be a living hope. May Peter rest in peace. Amen.

(ii) The Suffering and Silence

Our key word today is remember. We are about to be given
a period of silence in which to remember. How you use that
silence will very much determine the value of what we do
today. How do you plan to use it? Words and music have
helped us. But what will you do when there are no words
and music? When you are on your own?

May I make a suggestion? Remember as the Hebrews understood that term. Do not just look back to events long
before you were born – try and remember GCSE course work
and bad films: remember as the Hebrews did by putting yourself there. Think of the noise, the stench, the indecencies, the
sheer horror – imagine as my father once described to me
the necessity of shooting a comrade to put him out of his misery, and then writing a very different account of his death to
his parents. Imagine shooting the man who would not go
over the top that the others might and be shot as well.

Our silence should be a silence of bleakness, blankness,
hopelessness. And what then? Its Remembrance Sunday,
and every Sunday is a celebration of resurrection – that
through torture, pain and death, through that blood-stained
cross, new life breaks in. It doesn't happen without the
suffering: it happens through it. And then having made the
suffering our own, make that new life your own too. Determine today that your response will be to ensure that the
suffering of those men whose names are recorded in our
undercroft shall not have been in vain: that within this
school, your home, your house, your study a willingness for
peace prevails. Peace in the Hebrew sense of shalom –
harmony, wholeness, holiness

For if we are to build new attitudes which prevent the
costly follies of the past from being re-enacted – if we are to
learn from history, we must start where we are – in Senior
Common Room and JCR, at home and in house, at work
and in play, but first in silence.

9
BEREAVEMENT

*For me, saying goodbye is one of the hardest of things –
particularly from those one loves. Every goodbye is in
effect a bereavement, especially when it involves a
change of ministry. The final sermon of this collection
was preached when at fifty, I resigned my Oxford fellowship and became Headmaster of The King's School,
Canterbury. Many of my friends could not understand
such apparent folly!*

UNLESS a wheat grain falls into the ground and dies, it
remains only a single grain; but if it dies, it yields a rich
harvest.

I have never liked the end of the academic year. For seven-
teen years as an Oxbridge Chaplain I have had to suffer
annual bereavement as men, and latterly men and women,
whom I loved left College for the world outside. Of course
many have gone on to be close friends, and there was no
happier evening this term than when so many of my old
pupils came back for supper with Vicky and me. But there is
always a risk in parting, the risk that one may not meet
again, or worse still that when one does meet, personalities
will not be the same, and what had once been a natural
intimacy has become a necessary formality. Yet as pastor I
know no more pathetic condition than the man or woman
who cannot leave, who hangs on, fearful of what lies
beyond, unwilling to embrace maturity, ever seeking the
safety of the playpen. We have to let go, for what God calls

us to is not so much to do anything but to be. And being always involves becoming. Life, as Shakespeare's seven ages of man proclaims, is a journey, and those who will not travel will not know what it is to live.

Now the boot is on the other foot, for along with some of you, I too must depart. A journey beckons for me. Many of my colleagues have found it hard to understand why it is necessary. Oxford offers the don who is priest so much. There is the time for academic work, the time to be pastor – even if the tensions make it seem at times that one is bad at both. But there comes a time too when one knows instinctively that where one is there can be no more becoming, when another's gifts must be applied to the situation if that situation is again to be creative. Staying on is an admission of defeat, a saying no to what might be, an allowing what is, to stultify and stagnate. As Jesus himself knew, it can be good to go away.

But that does not make it easy. Looking round this chapel so many memories flood in – of joy and darkness, of tears and laughter, of the struggle to believe, and of the affirmation of belief. For this has not been a chapel in which those who worshipped have sought an easy faith. Together we have ventured on our own theological journeys, not afraid to risk, but conscious that the God who is creativity bids us ever venture, that we may know more of the truth which His Spirit wills to reveal. This has not been a chapel for retreating from the agonies of a perplexed and divided world, but one in which those who confessed did so amid all the doubts, ambiguities and tensions which no honest Christian can deny. Security has not been our watchword, but abandonment. We have indeed made our text our motto: 'Unless a wheat grain falls into the ground and dies, it remains only a single grain; but if it dies, it yields a rich harvest.' One of you said of my future work: 'Anthony, I hope you do for them what you have done for us: refuse to confirm our prejudices.' No better summary of what I hoped I had achieved could have been given. I am more than conscious that there have been many Christians in this College who could not follow where we have gone, and that has been a constant wound which I have had to bear, more painful than they ever imagine. But that has been the necessary cost of my discipleship, for there must be those who are willing to be at the frontiers of faith, or faith itself will degenerate into that comfortable irrelevance which it is for the majority of this College.

And we who struggle to confess must ever have in mind those who have not joined the struggle, who daily pass this Chapel which for over 400 years has stood at the centre of this College proclaiming the possibility of belief and inviting entry. Its witness has never been strident, nor cheap. It is perhaps best characterised by the daily worship where two or three are gathered together. But it has ensured a continuity of faith which at the end of the day has made and makes possible a vision which gives a dignity to life as nothing else can do.

For over eleven years, God has allowed me to be the enabler of His grace in this place in the administration of His sacraments. As pastor I have shared the doubts, despair, anger and hurt of generations of students. I have witnessed success and failure, seen the impossible become possible, opportunities thrown away. I have known both rejection and love. And like those to whom God called me to minister I too have had my doubts, and despair, I have been angry and hurt, I have enjoyed success and suffered failure, seen the impossible become possible, and thrown opportunities away. As minister of His grace, I know my utter dependence on that grace which I receive in the sacrament of penance. But it is not our failures which prevent the coming of the kingdom: God provides a way for dealing with them. It is our refusal to risk.

But a faith which proclaims that God is love must risk, for risk is the very essence of love. To abandon oneself to the other is the most risky thing one ever does, provides the biggest opportunity for hurt there can be. God risked in His creation of man, and suffers both the love and hurt that results. So as the community of love in this place, we have risked, risked showing that love for each other, risked where our communion would take us. We acknowledge our failures as week by week we gather for Eucharist, to be pardoned by Him who again sends us out to risk for Him. And that will be our endless journey wherever God sends us. If through my ministry I have encouraged others to that journey, then for all my failures, I count myself blessed by God.

It is not easy to talk about the will of God, and those who do it easily, cheapen Him. When an opportunity presents itself, and you have to decide what to do, it is rare indeed that you can ever be certain of the way ahead, can be sure that God is in it. For my part there has been much struggle and after the decision made, uncomfortable cold feet. I have never been very good at waiting on station platforms and protracted goodbyes are a sophisticated form of torture. I will not pretend that I can know that I am doing God's will. God does not in my experience give us those certainties. I believe it is a risk in which I pray I may find His presence.

A priest moving on not only leaves people whom he loves, but the building which has been the very vehicle of his ministry and which becomes part of his most intimate self. I shall miss this chapel more than words can express. When I came from the Chapel at Trinity Hall – described in the guide books as a small drawing-room – to the much larger St John's, I was not at once bowled over by it. No one could claim that what we see around us is a gem. However, it has over the years come to mean everything to me and I dread the last time I shall leave those doors as Chaplain, for it will then become part – as it should become part – of another priest's personality. It will never again be the same for me. If you have ever left a house you loved you will know something of what I am saying. Of your charity do not invite me back too soon.

And what of you, you whom I love. Some of you know that it was reading Bonhoeffer's *Cost of Discipleship* which finally decided me to offer myself for ordination. In my blackest moments, I always return and read it and draw strength to continue. So it is with Bonhoeffer that I want to leave you. May God bless you in your several ministries, may you ever have the courage to risk, may you never be afraid of being vulnerable, may you laugh and weep wholeheartedly, may you ever die that you may become, become an invitation to others to follow you on the journey of becoming. Bonhoeffer writes: Nothing can fill the gap when we are away from those we love, and it would be wrong to try and find anything. We must simply hold out and win through. That sounds very hard at first, but at the same time it is a great consolation, since leaving the gap unfilled preserves the bond between us. It is nonsense to say that God fills the gap: He does not fill it, but keeps it empty so that our communion with another may be kept alive, even at the cost of pain.